Henry VIII

Henry VIII

The charismatic king
who reforged a nation

Kathy Elgin

This edition published in 2020 by Arcturus Publishing Limited
26/27 Bickels Yard, 151–153 Bermondsey Street,
London SE1 3HA

AD007730UK

Printed in the UK

CONTENTS

CHAPTER ONE

AN UNEXPECTED CROWN

Although Henry VIII is perhaps England's most famous, or notorious, monarch, he should never really have been king at all. He was born on 28 June 1491, the second son and third child of King Henry VII and his queen, Elizabeth of York. It was his older brother Arthur who, as the eldest male child, was set to inherit the crown on the death of their father.

Arthur's birth in September 1486 had been eagerly awaited and was greeted with national rejoicing and a good deal of ceremony. That the first royal child was a son who would ensure the succession was always good news, as Henry himself would discover to his cost when he became king. In this case, after all the years of unrest in England during the Wars of the Roses, it was especially important that the new Tudor dynasty should be properly established.

Three years later, in 1489, the birth of Arthur's sister Margaret was also marked with much pomp and celebration, culminating in a fine christening in Westminster. Young Henry, by contrast, came into the world with very little publicity. He was born at Greenwich

Palace, down the river from Westminster and considered to be one of the king's 'out of town' residences. Built by Humphrey of Gloucester in 1447, Greenwich was the principal royal palace for 200 years. Originally known as Bella Court, it was renamed the Palace of Placentia (or Pleasaunce) by Margaret of Anjou, queen to Henry VI.

Henry did not receive the kind of attention his siblings had had. His grandmother, who recorded all the important family events in her bible, barely mentions Henry's arrival, whereas the births of the two older children are recorded in great detail, down to the exact time ('in the morning afore one of the clock after midnight', in Arthur's case).

This first known picture of Henry VIII shows a sturdy toddler with a mass of curly hair that we know from other sources to have been reddish-gold. Already out of baby clothes, he wears a tunic and has a gold chain.

However, being born the second son had its advantages. While Arthur was groomed for kingship right from the start, Henry enjoyed a more informal childhood and was allowed more freedom. He grew up with his sister Margaret in the royal nursery at Eltham, where they were soon briefly joined by three more sisters and a brother, of whom only one, Mary, survived childhood. When she came into the world in 1496, the family was still mourning the death of Elizabeth, a second daughter who had died aged three just six months before. A third son, Edmund, was born in 1499, but the little prince lived for less than eighteen

months. In 1503 Queen Elizabeth gave birth to another daughter, Katherine, but this child survived for only a few days. Childbirth was a dangerous business in those days, and most families, rich and poor alike, were used to the early deaths of children. For the royal family, it was a cause of constant anxiety as well as sadness, as they were only too aware that the succession depended on the survival of healthy male children.

KING ARTHUR

King Arthur was the fabled king of the ancient Britons who set up his court and the Round Table fellowship of knights at Camelot. The legends of King Arthur were widely known in Tudor times and many people believed him to have been real. The site of Camelot was thought to be the city of Winchester in southwest England. Henry VII, who was both superstitious and shrewd, made arrangements for his new son and heir to be born and christened in that ancient town. He also named him after King Arthur. In this way he hoped to give the new Tudor dynasty authenticity by linking it to the ancient line of British kings.

Henry, therefore, spent most of his life with his two sisters and in the company of his mother, who was a gentle and affectionate woman. Royal children often had a fairly distant relationship with their parents, but Queen Elizabeth is said to have taught her son to read and write, and they remained close throughout Henry's childhood. Perhaps it was growing up as the only boy in this unusually feminine environment that helped to mould Henry's later character. Not only

A panorama of the River Thames in 1543 reveals how buildings clustered in a strip along the north bank. The Palace of Whitehall, with its landing stage, can be seen on the left, with Westminster Abbey behind and further left. The building with a spire on the right is old St Paul's Cathedral.

was he clearly attractive to women, but he appears to have enjoyed and been happy in their company in a way that was unusual in the testosterone-fuelled Tudor society. On the other hand, he was undoubtedly spoiled and cosseted and became used to getting his own way.

TROUBLE IN THE FUTURE

The descendants of Henry's two surviving sisters were to be the cause of a good deal of trouble in later generations. His younger sister Mary was married to King Louis XII of France when she was just eighteen and he was 52. When he died, she secretly married Charles Brandon, Duke of Suffolk, against the wishes of her brother. After Henry's death, their granddaughter, the tragic Lady Jane Grey, became Queen of England for just nine days before being executed in 1554. Henry's older sister Margaret married King James IV of Scotland and became the grandmother of Mary, Queen of Scots. Mary's claim to the English throne was to prove a great threat to peace during the reign of Queen Elizabeth I.

INTO THE SPOTLIGHT

In 1494, when he was just three years old, Henry found himself suddenly thrust into public view when his father decided to give him the title Duke of York. This was prompted by recent events, which had threatened Henry VII's claim to the throne. A young man named Perkin Warbeck had appeared, claiming to be Richard, Duke of York, the younger of the two 'Princes in the Tower'. These were the two sons of Edward IV, who were thought to have been murdered by their uncle, Richard III, so that he could claim the crown. If Perkin

Henry VII founded the Tudor dynasty, forged trade agreements with other European countries and rebuilt the royal finances.

Warbeck could be proved to be the real prince, his claim to the throne would be much stronger than Henry's – and would be a serious threat to the Tudor dynasty. Warbeck was supported by many powerful figures in the courts of Europe, particularly by Margaret, Dowager Duchess of Burgundy, Edward IV's sister and therefore the young princes' aunt. King Henry needed to distract attention from all this until Warbeck could be exposed as a fake. He decided to create a real Duke of York and show him to the people in one of the greatest demonstrations of power and magnificence that England – and Europe – had ever seen.

PERKIN WARBECK

Having made his first claim to the throne from Burgundy in 1490, Warbeck landed in Ireland the following year in the hope of rallying supporters. When this failed, he returned to France where he was sheltered by the Duke of Burgundy and recognized by many as 'King Richard IV of England'. After a failed invasion of England in 1495, he fled again to Ireland and then Scotland, where he gained the support of King James IV. Both Scotland and Ireland were continually at odds with England and, as Warbeck

knew, could be counted on to look kindly on her enemies. When a planned Scottish invasion also failed, Warbeck returned to Ireland but by September 1497 he was back, this time finally landing on English soil in Cornwall. This was an area of England with a grievance against King Henry and Warbeck met with a warm welcome. He was declared Richard IV and raised an army of 6,000 men to march on London. King Henry immediately sent troops to intervene, and at their approach Warbeck lost his nerve. He deserted his army and was captured and interrogated, while the ringleaders of the plot were hanged. Warbeck was imprisoned in the Tower of London after being 'paraded through the streets on horseback amid much hooting and derision of the citizens'. The king hoped to dispel any remnants of support for the pretender. Warbeck did manage to escape from the Tower, but was soon recaptured and this time carried to execution tied to a cart.In November 1499 he was taken from the Tower to Tyburn, the place of execution, where he read out a confession and was hanged. Despite his ignominious end, many continued to believe that he had been the real Duke of York, or at least an illegitimate son of Edward IV, whom he much resembled.

The ceremony began with a parade in which the aristocracy of England, in their finest robes, rode through the streets and entered the City of London. They were led, astonishingly, by the three-year-old Prince Henry riding all by himself on a huge warhorse. This must have been quite a challenge for such a small child, but Henry apparently met it with confidence, as he did the rest of this gruelling ceremony. At Westminster a grand banquet was prepared, at which

Henry played the part of a squire waiting on his father. Next, before he could be created duke, Henry had first to be made a Knight of the Bath. He and the twenty or so gentlemen who were also being dubbed knight were undressed and given a ritual bath before being clothed in a rough hermit's gown and led to the chapel. There they kept vigil through the night before making confession and hearing mass, finally retiring to bed for a few hours' sleep just before dawn. In the morning they took to their horses again, riding round the palace yard before entering the hall where the knighting ceremony took place. Once a knight, Henry could officially receive the title of Duke of York from the king. Afterwards, in his new robes and coronet, he was carried round Westminster Hall by his father. This, the court recorder noted, was 'the best ordered and most praised of all the processions that I have heard of in England.'

Henry VII had pulled off an astonishing coup by stage-managing this ceremony. Even if the Warbeck threat had not been quite dismissed, he had seen his younger son make his first steps on the public stage. For the new Duke of York himself, it was his first taste of fame: he was emerging from the shadow of his brother Arthur as a character in his own right.

EDUCATION

Life, however, even for a prince, was not all ceremony and excitement. Henry also had to acquire an education. He may have learned to read and write at his mother's knee, but the man who proudly claimed to have taught the future king 'to spell' was his first private tutor, John Skelton.

Skelton was a poet, scholar and ordained priest, well versed in the classics, whose own poetry was often sharply satirical and sometimes rather improper. Educated at Oxford and Cambridge, John Skelton was already a kind of poet laureate when he found a patron in Henry's grandmother, the Countess of Richmond. Under her patronage he wrote elegies on the death of Edward IV and other royal figures, which was enough to bring him into the circle of the royal family and later make him a candidate for the tutorship of the young Henry. After he left Henry's service, Skelton was to find himself frequently in trouble with the authorities after satirizing corrupt clergy and political figures of the day in his poetry. With his lively mind and quirky imagination, he was a stimulating companion for the young prince. At his side Henry gained a firm grounding in Latin and also perhaps his taste for more contemporary works like Skelton's own. In addition to academic teaching, the prince's tutor was expected to mould his pupil's general behaviour; with this in mind, in 1501, Skelton presented Henry with a book of instruction entitled *Speculum principis! (Mirror for a Prince)*, one of many such handbooks which attempted to set down how a just and modern ruler should behave. Although little of this advice was revolutionary, the general effect of those early, impressionable years spent with John Skelton cannot be underestimated.

In the schoolroom, a boy's education consisted mainly of translating from Latin and Greek, grammar, rhetoric (the art of speaking and writing), logic, philosophy, arithmetic and geometry. He would also have studied history, which in those days did not distinguish much between factual chronicles of important events, such as those written down by monks, and the exploits of mythical kings and heroes told in songs and poetry. This was stimulating stuff for an imaginative boy and Henry soon became obsessed with chivalric tales, such as those of King Arthur and his knights.

In 1499 the royal children received a visit from one of the most famous men in Europe. The Dutch scholar Erasmus was staying at Greenwich while on a visit to England and was taken by his friend Thomas More to call on the royal family at nearby Eltham Palace. He recalled later his first meeting with the royal children: 'When we came to the hall, all the retinue was assembled. ... In the midst stood Henry, aged nine, already with certain royal demeanour; I mean a dignity of mind combined with a remarkable courtesy. On his right was Margaret, about eleven years old, who afterwards married James, King of the Scots. On the left Mary was playing, a child of four. Edmund was an infant in arms.'

THOMAS MALORY AND LE MORTE D'ARTHUR

While he was in prison in the early 1450s Sir Thomas Malory compiled a collection of the chivalric tales of King Arthur and his Knights of the Round Table. It took him twenty years. He collected the various English stories, translated French versions and almost certainly added some of his own. Together, the 21 parts of Le Morte d'Arthur (The Death of Arthur) tell the whole story, from the mysterious birth of Arthur to his death and the end of the Fellowship. In between are the tales of Lancelot and Guinevere, the Quest for the Holy Grail and many accounts of knightly adventures. The first printing in 1485 proved hugely popular, and two more editions followed in 1498 and 1529. The inscription at the end of the first edition reads:

'I pray you all gentlemen and gentlewomen that readeth this book of Arthur and his knights, from the beginning to the

ending, pray for me while I am alive, that God send me good deliverance and when I am dead, I pray you all pray for my soul. For this book was ended the ninth year of the reign of King Edward the Fourth by Sir Thomas Maleore, knight ...'

When Prince Henry was a boy, Malory's book was still quite new and it made very exciting reading for an imaginative youngster. It is said to have been Henry's favourite book. These stirring tales not only fired his boyish imagination but instilled in him romantic ideas about chivalry that stayed with him throughout his life. It was Malory, too, who first inspired Henry's love of tournament as a way of displaying manly courage. Although Caxton's early editions of *Le Morte d'Arthur* were not illustrated, the tales have been re-imagined by artists throughout the ages, including the Pre-Raphaelite Edward Burne-Jones and, here, Howard Pyle.

Erasmus was clearly impressed by his first encounter with the nine-year-old Henry and this admiration for Henry continued into his adult life. He later described Henry as having 'a lively mentality which reached for the stars, and he was able beyond measure to bring to perfection whichever task he undertook.' The admiration was clearly mutual, although the visit to Eltham narrowly avoided a diplomatic incident. Erasmus later recalled that Thomas More had simply suggested that they take a walk and call in at the palace. 'I had been carried off by Thomas More, who had come to pay me a visit on an estate of Mountjoy's where I was staying, to take a walk by way of diversion as far as the nearest town (Eltham). For there all the

royal children were being educated, Arthur alone excepted, the eldest son.' On arrival, however, he was taken aback to see More present Henry with the gift of his latest writing. Erasmus, unprepared and having nothing with him to offer, made an excuse and promised to send something in the future. Later in the evening when they were at dinner, Henry sent him a note reminding him of his promise. Three days later Erasmus, acting 'partly out of shame and partly out of vexation', delivered a new poem, accompanied by a letter addressed 'To the most illustrious prince, Duke Henry.' This incident, while it reveals tremendous self-confidence on Henry's part, is intriguing. Was Henry just rather cheekily demanding the tribute that he felt his position deserved, or was he genuinely keen to have something of his own from this eminent scholar? And was Erasmus merely flattering, or did he really see the potential ruler in this precocious boy?

ELTHAM PALACE

Eltham, where Henry spent much of his childhood, was a pleasant palace in the countryside, a few miles from Westminster. Originally a private moated manor house, it had been a royal residence since its acquisition by King Edward II in 1305. Edward IV had made substantial improvements, including building the Great Hall in the 1470s. Henry was the last king to spend much time at Eltham. Later monarchs preferred the nearby Greenwich Palace, which was more easily reached by river, and Eltham went into a sad decline. By the 16th century it was a farm, and the Great Hall was used as a barn. The magnificent hammer-beam roof of Eltham Palace's Tudor Great Hall is the third-largest in England. The hall is virtually all that

remains of the palace, although fragments of other buildings remain visible around the gardens. Fortunately, the Hall was rescued and, thanks to restoration, can still be seen today.

KING IN WAITING

Erasmus's description of the royal family assembled to greet him at Eltham is charming. It is also poignant, because that happy family was soon to see tragic changes. As Erasmus notes, the one character missing was, of course, Prince Arthur. While the younger children were enjoying each others' company and the comforting presence of their mother, Arthur was being groomed for kingship right from the start. Like Henry, he had been created a Knight of the Bath at the age of three, and then invested as Prince of Wales. He was given his own separate apartments and household of servants, and he grew up barely knowing his brothers and sisters. He had a rigorous education and was tutored by John Rede, headmaster of Winchester College, and later the blind French poet Bernard André. He was, to all accounts, a quiet and studious boy. Then, at the age of six, he was sent away from the court to Ludlow Castle, on the Welsh border, where the serious training for his future role began.

Henry's household

Both Arthur and Henry had their own households which were like the adult court in miniature. The princes had courtiers to wait on them, sometimes youngsters who were not much older than themselves, who grew up alongside them. Many of Henry's attendants became trusted friends and remained close to him for life. One of the more unusual juvenile appointments was that of the whipping boy. This was

In Holbein's portrait of Desiderius Erasmus, the scholar is shown alone in his study, his serenity and finely featured face cleverly suggesting his intellectual refinement.

a boy of the prince's own age whose job it was to take the punishment whenever the prince misbehaved. Because a prince was considered to be chosen by God, it followed that only God could punish him, so for minor offences, someone else had to be beaten instead. As the prince and his whipping boy grew up together, they often formed a kind of friendship. This was supposed to have a beneficial effect on the prince's behaviour, because (in theory, at least) the sight of his friend being whipped for something the prince had done would deter him from misbehaving again. Whipping boys were usually the sons of minor nobility, and although they may not have enjoyed the beatings, they were often rewarded in later life for their services.

A ROYAL BRIDE

Royal children were, of course, accustomed to having their whole lives mapped out for them, especially in the matter of marriage. Almost from the moment of his birth, Arthur's parents had been casting about for a suitable bride. They eventually settled on Katherine, the youngest daughter of Ferdinand of Aragon and Isabella of Castile, the joint rulers of Spain. The children were betrothed at the age of two, but Katherine's parents were in no hurry to send their daughter to England to meet her husband. Although this was a suitable political alliance, they may have been holding back in the hope of a better match. After all, the general view among European royal families was that Henry's position was not a strong one. The support gained by Perkin Warbeck had already proved that his claim to the throne could easily be challenged. Nevertheless, when Arthur reached the age of thirteen, he and Katherine were married by proxy in London, with the bride being represented by the Spanish ambassador. Katherine herself did not arrive in England for another two years, landing in the autumn of 1501.

This is one of only two authenticated portraits of Prince Arthur, seen here in 1500, just two years before his death. He seems a pale and reserved youth, unlike his solid, confident younger brother.

Arthur and Katherine had been writing to each other since their betrothal, but as they wrote in Latin and under the supervision of their respective schoolmasters, the letters were formal and hardly romantic. When they finally met, they were still virtual strangers. Even worse, their different pronunciation of Latin, the only language they had in common, meant that they could not understand each other. It was not an auspicious start, but Arthur wrote to his parents-in-law that he 'was immensely happy to behold the face of his lovely bride' and would be 'a true and loving husband.'

Ten days later, on 14 November 1501, they were married at St Paul's Cathedral. Young Henry, then a sprightly ten-year-old, was Katherine's escort throughout the ceremony and the evening celebrations, where he apparently stole the show with a display of nimble dancing. After the festivities, Arthur and his new bride returned to Ludlow to take up their married life. With this new, happy little family finally settled, it looked as though the Tudor

The young Katherine of Aragon already had a distant connection with England. She was named after her maternal great-grandmother Catalina who, before marriage to the King of Castile, was Catherine of Lancaster, daughter of John of Gaunt.

succession was all but secure. All they had to do was wait a year or so for the children to come along, and if Arthur was as lucky as his father, the first would be a son. But things did not go according to plan. Just five months later both the newly-weds were taken ill with the dreaded 'sweating sickness' and, although Katherine managed to survive the attack, Arthur did not. Within hours the heir to the throne was dead.

Sweating sickness

The sweating sickness was an illness much feared in the 15th and 16th centuries. It was quite different from the various forms of plague that swept through Europe around the same time, although it killed almost as many people. It first broke out in England at the beginning of Henry VII's reign in 1485 and reappeared on and off until the 1550s, when it disappeared as mysteriously as it had started.

The first symptoms were shivering and giddy spells, with pains in the neck and upper limbs, followed by sweating and a raised pulse rate. Sufferers also experienced severe thirst and cried out continually for water. They then fell into an exhausted sleep and died, usually within hours. People were especially afraid of this sickness because it had no outward symptoms, no boils or blisters such as plague victims suffered. Hardly anyone survived an attack of the sweating sickness and because its progress was so swift, there was no known treatment. Today, sweating sickness is thought to have been a form of typhus or possibly cholera. Either way, its causes were almost certainly polluted water and the generally overcrowded and unsanitary conditions in which people lived.

A NEW HEIR

Arthur's death threw the court into consternation. Apart from the king and queen's personal tragedy, it wasn't certain whether Arthur and Katherine had consummated their marriage. If they had, Katherine might already be pregnant with a future heir. This question would of course rise to haunt both Katherine and Henry in later years, but for now rumours were rife. Some of the Ludlow household maintained that Arthur had boasted about his sexual prowess, and of feeling 'lusty and amorous', while others repeated Katherine's denial that intercourse had ever taken place. Whatever the truth of this, it was eventually established that Katherine was not pregnant. Henry awoke to find that he was the heir apparent.

Despite this change in his prospects, Henry's life at first went on much as before. He was allowed to remain at Eltham, rather than following Arthur's path to Ludlow, but his education became more formal. His old tutor and companion, John Skelton, had already been replaced by John Holt, a professional schoolmaster. Holt's approach to Latin was considered rather more up-to-date than Skelton's and he had written an important textbook on grammar. When Holt died, William Hone took his place. More advanced subjects such as astronomy, navigation and map-making were added to the curriculum. Knowledge of these practical subjects would be very useful to Henry in later life when he took charge of the navy. There were other specialist teachers, too, to instruct him in modern languages, music and the martial arts, as well as a whole team of clerics to oversee his religious instruction.

Much as he enjoyed the company of his sisters, as Henry approached his teens he was drawn to the company of other boys of his own age who shared his love of physical sports – riding, jousting, tennis, archery and hunting. He excelled at these and was an enthusiastic opponent, although it was a brave boy who dared to beat him. Skilled as he was, Henry was not allowed to take part in the more dangerous feats of jousting; this filled him with frustration.

THE POWER OF PROPHECY

The medieval mind set great store by prophecies, astrology and the power of religious relics. The king's belief in these things was as strong as that of the poorest of his subjects. For example, all royal children had horoscopes cast at their birth. Predictions were not always accurate, however. In 1503 an Italian astrologer presented Prince Henry with a set of predictions as a New Year's gift. As well as giving an astrological explanation for the death of Prince Arthur, he predicted that Henry would enjoy a long and

happy reign and would have many sons. He also foretold a long life for Queen Elizabeth, who would live until she was 90. All these prophecies may have been what the royal family wanted to hear, but they proved sadly wrong.

FATHER AND SON

Barely had the family recovered from the loss of Arthur when another terrible blow hit. Less than a year after his death, Queen Elizabeth died giving birth to a daughter, Katherine. The baby also died a few days later. The death of an elder brother he had hardly known may not have affected Henry unduly, but the loss of his mother was devastating for the eleven-year-old. The king, too, was crippled by this loss. Although their marriage had been an astute political alliance, it had also been based on genuine affection. In his loneliness, the king turned his attention at last to his surviving son. Up till then he had paid Henry little attention. Henry's cousin Reginald Pole even hinted that the king had never really liked his second son, 'having no affection or fancy unto him'. Even when he became Prince of Wales, no ceremony had been organized to mark the occasion, whereas Arthur's investiture had been a grand and solemn affair. For the past year, it was as if in mourning the loss of his elder son, the king had forgotten he still had another. However, Elizabeth's death, and perhaps thoughts of his own mortality, galvanized him.

To mark the queen's death, Thomas More wrote *A Rueful Lamentation*. In this poem, Elizabeth bids farewell to her husband and children, wishing them well for the future they must face without her. She reminds the king that he must now be both father and mother to his children:

'Adieu mine own dear spouse, my worthy lord,
The faithful love that did us both combine,
In marriage and peaceable concord
Into your handes here I clean resign,
To be bestowed upon your children and mine.
Erst were you father, and now must you supply
The mother's part also, for lo now here I lie.'

The king appears to have taken this advice to heart. Prince Henry was taken from Eltham, almost the only home he had ever known, and installed in rooms adjoining his father's at Westminster. When the king and court left London to travel around the country, as it did at various times of the year, Henry went too, always accommodated in rooms adjoining his father's and with interconnecting doors. Their relationship suddenly changed from arm's length to an almost smothering closeness. From being a mother's boy, Henry was now his father's shadow. History does not reveal what he felt about this, but as father and son were of very different characters, it could not have been an easy relationship. At the age of 47, Henry VII was prematurely aged and his health was failing. His son was healthy, active and bursting with self-confidence. Virtually forbidden to associate with his old friends, he must have missed the familiar company of his sisters and other people of his own age. Living exclusively among the much older men who made up his father's court circle was stifling. In addition, Henry was hardly ever seen in public. The king's tactics during this period are hard to fathom. Was he afraid that his son might become too popular with the people, which he himself was not?

ELIZABETHA · VXOR
HENRICI · VII ·

Henry's mother, Elizabeth of York, was daughter, sister and wife of English monarchs. She was the eldest child of King Edward IV; her younger brother became king as Edward V; and in 1486 she became the wife of Henry VII. She did not live to see herself the mother of a king.

Henry VII would not have been the first king to worry about his people preferring a rival. In Shakespeare's play Richard II, the king speaks enviously of his rival Bolingbroke, and how he had:

> 'Observed his courtship to the common people;
> How he did seem to dive into their hearts
> With humble and familiar courtesy,
> What reverence he did throw away on slaves,
> Wooing poor craftsmen with the craft of smiles … '

FAMILY MAN

In January 1504 Henry was finally accorded public recognition as Prince of Wales in a ceremony at Westminster. The next step was to get him married. The obvious candidate was Katherine, who had been left in an awkward position following her young husband's death. She was a widow at seventeen, and stranded in a foreign country. King Henry was understandably keen to keep this valuable asset within his family and to safeguard his alliance with Spain, so negotiations were begun for Henry to be betrothed to his brother's widow. In June 1503 a marriage treaty was signed at Richmond Palace, but there were major obstacles, both religious and secular, standing in the way of this marriage. Under church law it was forbidden for a man to marry his brother's widow. In order for Henry to marry Katherine, they had to seek a special dispensation from the pope. This was to prove only the first of Henry's clashes with papal authority. To help secure this dispensation, Katherine testified that her marriage to Arthur had not been consummated, which meant that it was not valid in law.

HENRY VII: AN INSECURE KING

Henry VII was always aware that his grip on the throne might be threatened. He had not inherited the crown by natural succession, but had won it by defeating Richard III at the Battle of Bosworth in 1485. Then he had been 'Harry Tudor', son of Edmund Tudor, Earl of Richmond, and his wife Lady Margaret Beaufort. Both his parents had distant and slightly dubious claims to the throne. His father's father had been a commoner who had secretly married the widow of King Henry V; the union had produced four children. This meant that the Tudor claim to the throne was through the weaker, female line. His mother was descended from a grandson of Edward III who, because he was born before his parents' marriage, was considered illegitimate. Henry considered that winning his crown on the battlefield had given him greater entitlement than either of these distant connections, a view that was not shared by his enemies and rivals. Although the Wars of the Roses were over, there were still pockets of unrest around the country and there were many in the kingdom who felt they had a better claim to the throne.

More mundanely, there was the question of Katherine's dowry, which King Henry was anxious to keep and which had still not been paid in full. In addition, Henry was still only twelve years old. The treaty stated that he and the seventeen-year-old Katherine could not be officially married until his fourteenth birthday in June 1505. In 1504 it was confirmed that the pope was willing to grant the dispensation and the young couple were betrothed in a private ceremony. But shortly after this, news came that Katherine's mother, Queen Isabella, had died. This changed everything. With Isabella's death, her husband Ferdinand lost his title as King of Castile and with it his power and standing in Europe. Katherine's expected inheritance had mostly gone to her sister Joanna, who was now Queen of Castile. Katherine was no longer such a great prize, and King Henry called a halt to the marriage plans.

The unfortunate Katherine was now in an even worse position. She was still betrothed to Henry but could neither marry him nor go home to Spain. King Henry was still halfheartedly negotiating her dowry, while at the same time looking around for a better match for his son. For the next two years Katherine was kept a virtual prisoner at Durham House in London; she was close to the court but was rarely allowed to see her fiancé. The notoriously mean King Henry kept her short of money, which was a major concern because in addition to her own expenses she had to pay for the upkeep of her ladies-in-waiting. Pleading with the king to no avail, she wrote increasingly desperate letters home to her father, telling him of her plight and begging him to send her money. She had no decent clothes, she wrote, and was having to sell off some of her wedding silver in order to eat: 'I am in debt in London and this not for extravagant things … but only for food.'

Katherine was certainly used as a pawn in the game of international relations, but she was not to be underestimated. Some of her letters to her father suggest that she was quite aware of the game King Henry was playing: 'I choose what I believe, and say nothing. For I am not as simple as I may seem.' In 1507, still unmarried, she was acting as the Spanish ambassador to England, the first female ambassador in European history. In later life, throughout the long years of wrangling with Henry, she was to show the same spirit and determination.

THE DEATH OF HENRY VII

This impasse came to an end on 21 April 1509, when King Henry died of tuberculosis at Richmond Palace. A sketch drawn at the time shows Henry on his deathbed, surrounded by courtiers, physicians and priests. Death in those days was not a private affair. News of the king's death was not released for two days, while courtiers made hurried arrangements for the succession. There was always a chance that a pretender to the throne might appear, as Perkin Warbeck had earlier. But in the end, all went smoothly and on 23 April the seventeen-year-old Henry became King Henry VIII. After all the chaos of the Wars of the Roses, he was the first English king for almost a hundred years who had not had to take the crown by force or win it in battle.

After his father's funeral, one of Henry's first actions was to announce his intention to marry Katherine. It was now seven years since Arthur's death. Seven whole years during which she had been kept in enforced widowhood. Was Henry acting out of genuine affection, as the result of a promise made to his father on his deathbed, or guilt at the way Katherine had been treated? Or was it simply another wily attempt at international diplomacy? In this, as in all Tudor affairs, it is impossible to untangle the real motives. Whatever Henry's reasoning, he and Katherine were married quietly, on 11 June 1509, in a private chapel at Greenwich. Their joint coronation followed two weeks later, on 24 June. It was the biggest celebration England had seen.

MEMORIALIZING HENRY VII

The tomb of Henry VII and Elizabeth of York is in the Lady Chapel at Westminster Abbey. Henry planned this memorial to symbolize his establishment of the Tudor dynasty, commissioning one of the leading Italian sculptors, Pietro Torrigiani, to design it in a Renaissance style that is slightly at odds with the Gothic chapel in which it sits. A chronicler of the time commented: 'He lieth at Westminster in one of the stateliest and daintiest monuments of Europe, so he dwelleth more richly dead in the monument of his tomb than he did alive at Richmond in any of his palaces.' Henry and Elizabeth are also immortalized in a stained-glass window at Cardiff Castle. He is presented as lawgiver, she as faithful queen.

THE CORONATION

The day before, the royal couple had shown themselves to their people by going in procession through the city to Westminster. Both were magnificently dressed, and Katherine, true to the tradition of all brides of the period, wore her long hair down. Henry was resplendent in velvet and gemstones. The coronation itself, a long and solemn affair, was followed by a banquet and after this came days of feasting, dancing, masques and tournaments. As news of all this spread, it was clear the country was delighted with its new young monarch. After the tight-fisted parsimony of his father's reign, Henry was determined that his own would be one of magnificence, extravagance and pleasure. It must have felt as if the sun had suddenly come out. A flurry of celebratory odes and anthems from the cream of England's poets and musicians was presented to the king. Lord Mountjoy, writing to describe the great events to Erasmus, enthused: 'Heaven and earth rejoices; everything is full of milk and honey and nectar. Avarice has fled the country. Our king is not after gold, or gems, or precious metals, but virtue, glory, immortality …'

Henry VIII had started the way he meant to go on.

CHAPTER TWO

A RENAISSANCE PRINCE

The England that Henry VIII inherited was, thanks to his careful father, financially and politically stable, but it was not a country that felt good about itself. Despite having united the country and restored peace to England, Henry VII had not been popular, either as a leader or as a personality. He had restored financial stability and filled the country's coffers, left virtually bankrupt on the death of Edward IV, but only at the cost of alienating many of the nobility, who resented the stringent taxes and fines imposed on them and the ruthlessness with which laws were applied.

Henry and his father could not have been more different. Where the old king had been a cold fish, cautious, shrewd and penny-pinching, his son was ebullient, larger-than-life, reckless and extravagant. He was subject to sudden enthusiasms and equally sudden losses of interest, and this attitude applied to people as well as to activities.

THE LEGACY OF HENRY VII

Henry VII was not a military man and, unlike his predecessors, had no interest in making war with France or other European states, preferring to cement alliances by brokering treaties and trade agreements. Shrewd and frugal as he was, he must also have realized that war was an expensive business that England could ill afford. His constant dithering over the betrothal of Prince Henry to Katherine, and the Anglo-Spanish treaty it sealed, is a good example of his attitude to international relations.

Henry VII's biggest domestic problem had been the wealthy local families who maintained their power bases in various parts of the country and always represented a potential threat of unrest. These families controlled huge bodies of men who worked on their land and were officially recognized as servants or retainers. In fact, they amounted to private armies that could be raised at any moment to fight their neighbours or, in extreme circumstances, their king.

As long as they remained loyal to him, Henry was happy to allow the nobles a certain amount of local autonomy, but he took careful steps to keep them in line and to curtail their power. Laws were passed limiting the number of men they could retain, and against the wearing of 'livery', the badges and uniforms that denoted the retainers' family allegiance. He also appointed a network of justices of the peace to serve throughout the country, charged with maintaining the rule of law in their particular region. Although unpaid, justice of the peace was a position of great prestige and influence and it was much coveted. A less popular creation was the court of Star Chamber, an inner group of Henry's Privy Council with the power to overrule the legal system and settle any disputes that threatened the king's authority. People lived in fear of the Star Chamber, and the men who administered it.

REVENGE ON THE OLD GUARD

Two of the ministers most hated by the public were Sir Richard Empson and Sir Edward Dudley, who were seen as responsible for implementing the laws on taxation. These laws were seen by many as arbitrary and they were pursued with vigour by the Privy Council. Many believed that taxation under Henry VII and his advisers Sir Richard Empson and Sir Edward Dudley had been little more than financial looting. One of Henry VIII's first acts, just two days after his coronation, was to have Empson and Dudley arrested, tried for high treason and executed. Henry also returned to the public some of the money supposedly extorted by the two ministers: 'His executors made restitution of great sums of money, to many persons taken against good conscience to the said king's use, by the forenamed Empson and Dudley.' This was a shrewd move that immediately endeared the new king to his subjects.

THE END OF THE YORKIST THREAT

Another of Henry's early moves was to rid himself of the last remnant of the Yorkist threat which had so haunted his father. Edmund de la Pole, Duke of Suffolk, was the grandson of Richard Plantagenet, Duke of York, and the leading Yorkist claimant to the throne. Seeking the protection of the court of Burgundy, he had later been given up by them into the custody of Henry VII, who imprisoned him in the Tower. The old king had been content to leave him there, but his more businesslike son saw no reason to keep the threat alive and in 1513 he had Edmund executed.

Henry was not simply concerned with establishing popularity at home. He had his sights set much further afield and his aim was all-embracing. England in 1509 was still emerging from the late medieval period into a more modern world. The concentration on domestic affairs during the Wars of the Roses had kept the country somewhat isolated from the rest of Europe. As the great upheaval known as the Renaissance spread throughout Europe, knowledge and scholarship flourished hand in hand with social and political change under the impetus of radical thinkers and scholars. In Germany, Martin Luther and others had initiated the Reformation, freeing religion from what Luther saw as the tyranny and corruption of the Roman Catholic church. Thanks to his liberal education, and his cultivation of men like Erasmus who were at the forefront of the new thinking, Henry was very much aware of the currents of thought sweeping Europe. He realized that England needed to be part of this bright new world and saw it as his personal destiny to make a mark on Europe.

Sir Thomas More, ever ready with appropriate flattery, proclaimed at Henry's accession: 'This day is the end of our slavery, the fount of our liberty; the end of sadness, the beginning of joy.' But even More's eulogy could hardly have matched the ambition in Henry's own mind. He would position England as the foremost power in Europe, while he himself would become the most celebrated Renaissance prince, excelling all rivals.

THE PRINCE

The concept of the Renaissance prince derived largely from the chivalric literature of the earlier medieval period and was an all-embracing role. A prince had to embody not only the manly virtues of strength and courage but also, more elusive, those of a more social

nature. In war his courage and desire for victory should be tempered with nobility and grace towards the defeated; at home he should excel at sports while exhibiting fairness. He should be widely read, be able to converse in other contemporary languages as well as in Latin and possibly Greek, write poetry and music and play at least one instrument tolerably well. He should also be elegant in appearance, always well dressed in the finest fabrics and at the forefront of fashion, nimble on the dance floor and courteous, especially where women were concerned.

THE RENAISSANCE

The Renaissance was the flowering of arts and science throughout Europe during a period from roughly the late 14th century to the 17th century. Generally agreed to have begun in Florence in the 14th century, it spread first through the rest of Italy and then to other parts of Europe. In Italy, leading practitioners were artists such as Leonardo da Vinci, Raphael and Michelangelo, musicians such as Palestrina and scientists such as Copernicus and, later, Galileo. As well as this prolonged burst of creativity, the period saw enormous social change, thanks to revolutionary new thinking in the areas of politics and religion. However, the effects of all this were not experienced universally throughout Europe at the same time. In England, a comparative latecomer into this new world, the Renaissance can be considered as roughly contemporary with the age of the Tudors, encompassing the early writing of More and Spenser and the music of Tallis and Dowland, and reaching its high point with the work of writers such as Christopher Marlowe and, of course, William Shakespeare.

THE BOOK OF RULES

To help rulers achieve these attainments, the 16th century saw a fashion for 'courtesy books', manuals of conduct and good manners – the equivalent of today's 'self-help' books. Usually addressed to a particular patron, they represented useful, if predictably respectful advice on a good Christian ruler's duties towards God and his subjects, and how a young noble should conduct himself. They combined philosophical discourse with practical advice on everything from gentlemanly behaviour and courtesy towards women to dress sense and table manners. Written by courtiers who had had experience of observing rulers at close hand and ostensibly addressed to individuals, they were no doubt also intended for a wider audience in the hope that minor nobles might emulate their betters.

Two of the most influential came from Italy. Baldassare Castiglione's *Il Libro del Cortegiano (The Book of the Courtier)*, which appeared in 1528, drew on his years spent in the service of Guidobaldo da Montefeltro, Duke of Urbino, who presided over the most refined and sophisticated court in the whole of Italy at that time.

Machiavelli's *Il Principe (The Prince)*, on the other hand, was much more overtly political in its consideration of the role of a ruler and came to be regarded by many as scandalous and immoral, thanks to sections in which the author appeared to be advocating tyrannical behaviour. Born in Florence in 1469, Niccolò Machiavelli is considered as the founder of modern political science, although his works are often misinterpreted. Curiously, he was also the author of comedies, songs and poetry and a translator of classical works. The phrase 'the end justifies the means' is often used to sum up Machiavelli's thesis. Machiavelli dedicated *The Prince* to Lorenzo de' Medici, a member of one of the most magnificent and ruthless

many warring families in Florence, so perhaps his advice was
. Known as Lorenzo the Magnificent, Lorenzo de' Medici was
omat, politician and *de facto* ruler of the Florentine Republic,
aining a fragile peace between the squabbling Italian city-states.
ugh ruthless, he is best remembered as a great patron of the arts,
coinciding with the high point of the Italian Renaissance. *The*
was probably written around 1513, although it only appeared
t in 1532, after Machiavelli's death.

he fashion for the conduct book soon spread beyond Italy.
us's *Education of a Christian Prince*, written for the Habsburg
Emperor Charles V in 1516, struck a more humanitarian note than
some. Erasmus suggested that those charged with the education of
princes should be of high moral standing and a gentle disposition;
they should avoid corporal punishment and treat the student as an
individual. He advised the prince to seek knowledge in the classical
authors, with the caveat that they, unlike him, did not have the
benefit of Christianity. And with regard to kingship: 'Conduct your
own rule as if you were striving to ensure that no successor could be
your equal, but all the time prepare your children for their future
reign as if to ensure that a better man would indeed succeed you.'

These conduct books continued in popularity throughout the
16th century, and in 1599 King James VI of Scotland wrote his own
three-volume treatise for his son Henry, *Basilikon Doron* ('Royal Gift'
in Greek). Made more widely available in London in 1603 on James
VI's accession to the English throne, it sold thousands of copies.

THE BOOK OF THE COURTIER

Castiglione's book imagines a series of philosophical conversations
that take place over four leisurely evenings between young men at

Holbein's great portrait The Ambassadors *(1533) indicates the high standing of foreign ambassadors at court. They acted as go-between for heads of state and their journals and letters home are an invaluable record of crucial events. The figure on the left, in secular clothes, is Jean de Dinteville, the French ambassador to Henry's court in 1533. The other is Georges de Selve, Bishop of Lavaur, who frequently acted as ambassador on religious and political matters.*

the Court of Urbino, presided over by the Duchess Elisabetta and her sister. As they debate the meaning of love, service, attitudes to women and the nature of nobility, what emerges is a picture of the

perfect courtier. Translated into at least six languages, *The Book of the Courtier* was one of the most influential books of the Renaissance. It appeared in English in 1561, translated by Thomas Hoby, and immediately became the must-have book for the aspiring young bloods of Queen Elizabeth's court. Thanks to the detailed picture it gives of contemporary court life, it proved invaluable to historians and is still regarded as one of the most important works of the Renaissance.

SPREADING THE WORD

The invention of the printing press and moveable type was a major revolution in the dissemination of knowledge. It meant that books could be produced more quickly and in far greater number than under the old method of woodblock printing. Johannes Gutenberg had perfected the press in Germany around 1450, but it was the writer and diplomat William Caxton who introduced the printing press to England and became the first English retailer of books. Having studied printing in Bruges and published his first work there, Caxton returned to England and set up his first press in Westminster in 1476, producing an edition of Chaucer's *Canterbury Tales*.

During the next sixteen years he printed over a hundred books and was responsible for introducing a number of major classical works into English, many of which he translated himself. Printed books were still relatively expensive, however, and Caxton's patrons were mainly the upper classes. This was to change when Caxton died and his partner and successor Wynkyn de Worde, from Alsace, took over the business. De Worde was instrumental in producing less expensive books aimed at a mass market, and his work included everything from romances, poetry and books for children to volumes of advice on household management and farming, many of which were illustrated. A true innovator, Wynkyn de Worde was the first to start selling his books from a stall in St Paul's churchyard, which soon became a major centre for booksellers. In 1500 he was the first printer to set up in Fleet Street, beginning the long relationship of that street with British journalism and newspaper production.

MANNERS MAKETH MAN

Once books were more freely available in the public realm, the advice to princes filtered down through the ranks of the nobility. In essence, the Renaissance ideal is about presenting a good image of oneself: Renaissance man behaves always as if in front of an audience (which of course in the case of a ruler, he usually was). He should perform with a kind of natural grace, concealing any trace of the effort involved.

By general agreement, the courtier should have a beautiful speaking voice ('sonorous, clear, sweet and well sounding') in which he can articulate fine sentiments. He needs to possess a cool mind and immaculate appearance ('tempered by a calm face and with a play of the eyes that shall give an effect of grace'). He must appreciate the arts and be well versed in the classics and humanities. At the same time he should be athletic and have a 'warrior spirit', which should find expression in heroic deeds. Once he has perfected these virtues, he should use them for the general good or, in the case of princes, for the good of his subjects.

It's difficult to say how many of these books Henry was familiar with at first hand, since some of them almost certainly circulated in unpublished form before their actual date of publication. *The Book of the Courtier*, for example, was not published in English until many

Illustrations featuring scenes of jousting and knightly deeds were always popular, although this little scene from a book of hours or illustrated manuscript seems to show young men being trained in the art of tilting, rather than in actual combat.

years after Henry's death but it had been known and discussed in Italy since 1528 and may have been familiar by word of mouth in court circles. However, he certainly knew Machiavelli's *The Prince* and made use of it when contemplating his relationship with the Church of Rome. This kind of literature combined perfectly with the chivalric tales of adventure that Henry had loved in his childhood to suggest an ideal of manhood to which he strove to aspire.

THE OLD ORDER

However warmly the people of England welcomed their new monarch, and however much he dominated the court scene, when it came to politics Henry was not allowed to overthrow completely the network of administration upon which his father had depended. Many of the old government officials were still in place and would continue to block his reforms for years to come. In the early years of his reign, the Privy Council sought to oversee everything he did, insisting on countersigning documents as if he were not yet a ruler in his own right. The great families still maintained their power bases in various parts of the country. It would be several years before Henry could take the reins of government into his own hands and he may well have found these constraints frustrating. Perhaps this encouraged him to put most of his energies into his private life, which was, increasingly, a hectic round of pleasure.

HENRY THE SPORTSMAN

Always naturally athletic, now at seventeen Henry was beginning to look like his grandfather. He was handsome, tall, strong and, at this period, slender. It's hard to see, in the Henry of 1509, the bloated, stocky figure familiar from the later portraits. He had none of the studious look of his late brother Arthur, and certainly none of his quiet disposition. Henry was a tornado of activity. He liked nothing better than to be outdoors, enjoying some kind of physical activity with his coterie of young men. They rode, ran races, practised martial arts, jousted or fought with blunt swords, or held archery practice with long bows. If they had to be indoors, they played real tennis, a hard-hitting game that was played to win. Henry excelled at all these sports and cut a dashing figure. But what he really loved was hunting.

THE THRILL OF THE CHASE

Since medieval times, hunting was the prime sport of the aristocracy. As well as providing exercise and excitement in the thrill of the chase, it had always been regarded as a means of training men for warfare. The same strategies of stalking, pursuit and kill perfected on deer or foxes could just as easily be applied to enemy soldiers. Henry adored it, for all these reasons. He was often to be found in the hunting field when he should have been attending to his duties at court. In 1520 one of his courtiers reported wryly that 'The king rises daily, except on holy days, at four or five o' clock, and hunts till nine or ten at night. He spares no pains to convert the sport of hunting into a martyrdom.' Rumour had it that he frequently wore out eight horses in a day's sport. The favourite royal hunting grounds were at Richmond and around Greenwich in the vast areas of forest that still stood on the outskirts of London. The quarry was usually deer, which had from medieval times been the prerogative of the king: traditionally, anyone caught poaching deer could be executed. Smaller animals like fox or rabbit were left to the lower classes. The excitement of hunting lay in the chase, and the hart (a deer of at least six years of age) was considered the most prestigious target, being the

largest and most wily creature in the deer park. The venison yielded was usually given away – an opportunity for the host to display his beneficence. A different breed of dog was suited to each quarry – deerhounds, otterhounds, greyhounds for harecoursing, spaniels for retrieving and so on.

REAL TENNIS

Real, or 'royal', tennis was played on a stone indoor court and was a more solid affair than the game we know today. The ball was made of sheepskin stuffed with sawdust or wool and the racquets, strung with sheep-gut, had to be tightly and closely strung to cope with the heavy ball. Service was always from one end, where spectators sat, while the opposite end into which the ball was struck was known as the 'hazard'. Although players needed quick reactions and a certain amount of agility, the game demanded strength rather than the light touch perfected by tennis players today. The real tennis court at Hampton Court Palace is the oldest surviving court in England, and is thought to have been built in 1526.

Henry had indoor sports facilities built at Hampton Court, Greenwich and Whitehall, which boasted four real tennis courts, two bowling alleys, a cockpit and a tiltyard. An inveterate gambler, Henry could never resist a wager on the outcome of a tennis match, a joust or at cards.

TOURNAMENTS

The most popular entertainment in the Tudor period was the tournament. This was not just an exciting sporting occasion with thrills and spills, it offered scope for a diplomatic moment. Tournaments, with their pageantry and spectacle, offered an excellent opportunity

Real tennis, played on an indoor court, was the most popular means of keeping fit in bad weather. Henry played almost daily when he was at Hampton Court, and King Francis I of France was an enthusiastic player and builder of courts.

to impress foreign ambassadors, who could be trusted to carry home to their employers tales of the magnificence of the English court. When the king himself was involved, it was a chance to show off his personal strength and dominance. The man who unhorsed rivals in the jousting run was clearly not a man to trifle with in battle.

At the same time, the tournament was a kind of theatre in its own right. The allegorical tournaments staged in the Tudor period were a recreation of those organized at the court of the dukes of Burgundy a hundred years earlier, a conscious throwback to the age of chivalry and of medieval sophistication. Within the fictional framework, courtier-knights were engaged on a romantic quest, dressed as various allegorical figures. This visual representation of vice and virtue was an important element of the Tudor pageant and offered a great excuse for extravagant dressing up.

A typical tournament

Tournaments ran to a fixed agenda, and each day's events followed a set course. After the queens and spectators had taken their seats, a knight entered with a band of about a dozen challengers. They paraded around the lists, doing reverence to the queens and sometimes receiving favours from them. Then the answerers entered and did the same. The individual jousts then began, with heralds and judges keeping a tally of the scores.

Tilting was the main form of individual combat, in which the object was to break a lance on an opponent's shield. Blunt lances were used to avoid injury, but many contestants were wounded or killed in these combats. The tilting could continue for up to a week. After the tilt came the tourney course, which usually lasted for two days. The tourney was a contest between two groups of mounted combatants who normally first charged with lances and then fought with swords.

The system of scoring in a tournament was quite complex. The names of the challengers and defenders were listed in columns, with a rectangular box next to each name. In the box the outcome of each joust was recorded by diagrammatic marks, rather like today's ballet notation. A mark on one part of a line would indicate a strike to the opponent's head, a mark on another part meant a strike to the body, while yet another would indicate a lance successfully broken. Details of Tudor tournaments were carefully recorded and many have survived.

The 1511 tournament

The first of many grand tournaments organized by Henry was held at Westminster in 1511 to celebrate the birth of his first child. It was heralded by the issuing of an elaborate written challenge, signed by the king and listing the rules of the tournament along with an outline of the story.

This told how Queen Noble Renown, of the kingdom of Noble Heart, had sent four knights to England to joust against all comers in celebration of the birth of the royal prince. The names of the leading characters are derived from *The Romance of the Rose*, the greatest of the medieval romances. Cueur Loyal (Faithful Heart) was played by Henry, Vaillant Desyr (Valiant Desire) by Sir Thomas Knyvet, Bon Vouloir (Good Intentions) by Lord William Courtenay and Joyeux Penser (Happy Thoughts) by Sir Edward Neville, three of his foremost courtiers. Other courtiers signed up to answer the challenge.

On the day, no expense was spared in creating a spectacle to top anything that had gone before. The four challengers were trundled into the arena inside a moveable forest, which also contained a castle made from gold paper. Elaborate costumes, trappings for the horses and banners to hang from the walls were conjured up by the royal wardrobe.

In the actual jousting, it's not surprising to find that the score-sheet kept by the herald records King Henry as having the highest score, making three strokes on the body and breaking four lances. This may have been because, characteristically, he took part in more jousts than anyone else. Queen Katherine, however, declared that Sir Thomas Knyvet was the overall champion and awarded him the prize. Henry, on this occasion at least, seems to have been a good loser. Soon after the event, the tournament was illustrated

on a 60-foot-long vellum roll painted by the workshop of Thomas Wriothesley, Garter King of Arms. The various festivities and the notable celebrities who attended the event are clearly identifiable in this outstanding work of art.

Another tournament, held at Greenwich in 1517, was judged even more splendid. This time the event was held specifically for the entertainment of visiting foreign ambassadors and was clearly meant to be awe-inspiring. It began with the triumphal entry of a gorgeously-clad Henry, in gilded armour, leading a mounted procession of eleven challengers and 125 retainers. The contemporary chronicler Edward Hall was so overcome by the splendour of it all that he paid little attention to the actual tilting and didn't bother to record the scores. In fact, Hall's accounts of Henry's tournaments rather outweigh his reporting of more important events of his reign, which proves that these shows of power and magnificence had exactly the effect intended.

THE HOME FRONT

Splendid as the 1511 tournament was, it was also memorable for another, far less happy reason. Like his father, Henry was greatly concerned to secure the Tudor succession as soon as possible, so he had been delighted when, a few months after the coronation, it was confirmed that Katherine was pregnant. Sadly, this had ended in the stillbirth of a daughter in January 1510. The news that Katherine was pregnant again some four months later had revived their hopes, and when she gave birth to a son on New Year's Day, 1511, Henry decided to celebrate in style. The tournament was a great success but misfortune dogged the royal couple. Just a few days after the celebrations, little Prince Henry sickened and died, plunging his

parents into despair. This was to prove a grim forewarning of future events. Of Katherine's six children, including three sons, born during their marriage only one daughter, Mary, would survive.

These domestic tragedies must have brought back memories to haunt Henry of his own dead siblings and the death of his mother. In spite of this, the royal marriage was outwardly happy enough. Henry wrote several letters to his father-in-law, Ferdinand of Aragon, telling him how happy he and Katherine were, enthusing in one: 'as for that entire love which we bear to the most serene Queen, our consort – day by day do her inestimable virtues more and more shine forth, flourish and increase, so that even if we were still free, it is she, nevertheless, that we would choose for our wife before all other.' Katherine was a popular queen and for now at least Henry appears to have been reasonably faithful. While waiting for the longed-for son to come along, he busied himself with international politics.

A REAL-LIFE ROLE MODEL

Time and again in his early years, Henry had cast around for role models, aspiring to cement relationships with men he felt were worthy of emulation or against whom he could judge himself. His early, rather precocious attempt at cultivating Erasmus when he was just nine is perhaps the first of these. Throughout his life he was genuinely keen to learn from the best and sought to surround himself with what he considered to be good advisers.

At the age of fifteen, Henry had been appointed to escort the 28-year-old Philip the Fair, King of Castile, during his stay at the English court in 1506. Although Philip the Fair's time in England was providential in the sense that he and Prince Henry struck up a friendship, his arrival was, in fact, unintentional. He and his wife

Joanna were shipwrecked off the coast of Dorset on their way home to Spain and were virtually held hostage by Henry VII for their stay in England. They were only released after Philip had signed a treaty with the wily Henry that included a mutual defence pact, the release of English exiles under Philip's protection and a trade agreement highly preferential to English cloth merchants. Together Philip and Henry went to see the Round Table at Winchester, where they revelled in the knightly deeds of King Arthur. When they returned to the court of Henry VII, the rather dull business of diplomacy was enlivened by jousting and tennis matches, at which the handsome and athletic Philip easily saw off all the English champions. Henry seems to have seen in him an example for his own future kingship, and when Philip returned home, Henry wrote to him in the friendliest terms, asking that they should correspond regularly. Sadly, this was not to be. He was robbed of his new friend only a few months later, when Philip died suddenly from typhoid.

Sir Henry Guildford was one of Henry's favourite companions, richly rewarded for his military service in France and his diplomatic missions in the service of Thomas Wolsey. Even his strong opposition to Henry's divorce did not lose him the king's favour, although it made him an enemy in Anne Boleyn, who threatened that when she was queen she would remove him from his position as Comptroller of the Royal Household. He replied that he would sooner resign himself, but Henry refused to accept his resignation and twice made him take back his staff of office.

A WORD OF ADVICE

Flattery was one of the best known means of advancement at court. A headstrong character like Henry was a dangerous man to cross and few dared to risk disagreement with him. Councillors often found it politic to go along with what he had already decided. However, sometimes the king had to be told a few home truths. In 1513 Erasmus produced a new translation of Plutarch's 'How to tell a flatterer from a friend' from Greek into Latin and took the liberty of dedicating it to Henry. Realizing the potentially hazardous nature of what he was undertaking, Erasmus covered himself by pointing out delicately in his dedication that reprimanding a friend takes tact and diplomacy 'in case we undermine friendship itself even while we clumsily try to cure our friend's fault.'

Once Henry was king, however, there were opportunities for self-promotion on a world stage. His major rivals in this European drama were Francis I of France and Charles V, first King of Spain and subsequently Holy Roman Emperor.

FRANCIS I

Francis was King of France from 1515 until his death in 1547. He was Henry's almost exact contemporary and, like him, had come to the throne unexpectedly, in his case from a distant branch of the royal family. He was handsome, well educated and cut a dashing figure. In a country more inclined to war than to culture, he was a major patron of the arts, pulling off something of a coup by persuading the aged Leonardo da Vinci to spend his last years in France. He also enjoyed a reputation as a man of letters, considerably enlarging the royal library and writing poetry of his own. He spent a fortune on building or extending his many royal chateaux in new Renaissance architectural styles. The grandest of his projects was the chateau of Fontainebleau outside Paris, his favourite royal residence, which became one of the marvels of the age. An earlier chateau at Fontainebleau, near Paris, had been the favourite country residence of several French kings, but it was Francis I who turned the site into the first Renaissance palace in France. Francis commissioned the architect Gilles le Breton to design the palace and its grounds and even persuaded Leonardo da Vinci to advise.

Francis is one of the contemporary figures discussed in the conversations of *The Book of the Courtier*, where he emerges as the leader most likely to bring culture to France.

Anne Boleyn and her sister Mary were both sent to Francis' court as a kind of finishing school in 1514. Francis pursued a vigorous romantic life and had several mistresses – Mary Boleyn among them – some of whom were allowed to wield considerable power at court. It's quite possible that this was where Anne Boleyn acquired both her interest in politics and her way of managing royalty.

On the military front Francis was less successful, becoming embroiled in an ongoing and debilitating series of wars for supremacy in Italy. His sworn enemy was Charles V, with whom he enjoyed an intense personal rivalry that was played out throughout their lives, often to the detriment of their respective peoples. At the Battle of Pavia in 1525, Francis was ignominiously captured and imprisoned by Charles and forced to make concessions before being released.

CHARLES V

As the heir of not just one but three of the leading dynasties – the houses of Habsburg, Valois-Burgundy and Castile-Aragon – Charles was one of the most powerful men of the day. Born in Ghent in 1500, Charles V was the son of Philip IV ('the Handsome') of France and Joanna ('the Mad') of Spain and, as such, Katherine of Aragon's

Francis I was the one European monarch who, from his portraits, could rival Henry VIII in splendor. While the fine clothes embody wealth and power, he allows a slight knowing smile to play about his features.

nephew, although this only partially endeared him to England. While a great lover of peace, such was the expanse of his dominions that Charles was almost always at war.

By 1519, when he became Holy Roman Emperor, he controlled much of Europe as well as rich colonies in America and Asia. A highly cultured man who spoke several European languages, he was also a committed Catholic who held out against the Reformation. This brought him into conflict with Henry, with whom he had until then enjoyed a fairly amicable relationship and to whom, as Katherine of Aragon's nephew, he was related. Despite being at war, mostly against France, for most of his reign, Charles had a reputation as a lover of peace: 'not greedy of territory, but most greedy of peace and quiet', as he was described by the Venetian diplomat and diarist Marcantonio Contarini in 1536.

These, then, were the two high-profile rulers against whom Henry sought to measure himself. Over the next two decades their three-cornered rivalry saw treaties brokered and broken, alliances shifted and invasions threatened. Time and again Henry, Francis and Charles rubbed up against each other in war, in territorial disputes and in personal competition. The efforts of each one in building a new palace, acquiring a new work of art or conquering another stretch of land spurred the other two on to outdo him. This schoolboy desire for competition had results both positive and negative. In the cultural sphere it produced many exquisite buildings, paintings and literature, while on a practical level it swallowed up vast amounts of public money and it had a destabilizing effect: the citizens of Europe could have hardly ever known for sure whose side they were on in any given week, or with whom they might be expected to go to war.

THE HOLY ROMAN EMPIRE

The Holy Roman Empire was a loose union of territories covering much of central Europe. Having its origins in the ancient Frankish empire, it included what we now know as Germany, the Kingdom of Bohemia (now the Czech Republic), parts of northern Italy and the Kingdom of Burgundy (roughly southwest France). It took its name from an explicit and grandiose comparison with the original Roman Empire, which had covered the same area. By the 1500s it was sometimes known as the 'Holy Roman Empire of the German Nation', to reflect the fact that many of its Italian and Burgundian lands had been lost and the new importance of the German imperial estates.

Charles V had been Holy Roman Emperor for 14 years when this portrait was painted in 1533.

Holy Roman Empire of the German Nation was not a hereditary title, although the emperors came almost exclusively from the Habsburg dynasty. The new candidate was chosen by the votes of three archbishops and four secular princes, and was first given the title 'King of the Romans' or 'Emperor-elect of the Romans' until he was crowned by the pope. Charles V was one of the few who bothered to travel to Rome for a full papal coronation, thus being allowed to adopt the full title.

CHAPTER THREE

WAR AND PEACE

'The new king is eighteen years old, a worthy king and most hostile to France ... it is thought he will indubitably invade France.'

Venetian diplomat, 1509

Going to war was a prerequisite of European monarchs, as a way of holding on to territory, maintaining their country's supremacy, and as an indicator of their personal standing. One thing was expected of an English king, and it was that he would invade France and reclaim ancestral lands lost by previous generations. Barely had Henry settled in to his role as king and family man before he started casting his eyes across the Channel. After all those years of training in martial arts and hunting, he was more than ready for the challenge. In 1513, just four years into his reign, Henry went to war.

HEROES

In England, the heroes who encapsulated the chivalric values prized by the Renaissance included not only Henry's childhood favourite King Arthur and his Knights of the Round Table, but the more recent and real-life figures of King Henry V and the Black Prince, son of Edward III. Their deeds were told over in ballads and would have been well known even to the children of the common people. To a prince, they were inspirational. Henry V had won fame in the Hundred Years War, culminating in his celebrated victory against impossible odds at the Battle of Agincourt in 1415 before his early death at the age of 35 in 1422.

Edward III's eldest son, Edward of Woodstock, as he was called in early life, is more popularly known as the Black Prince and is traditionally thought to have acquired his nickname either from the suit of armour he wore or his black shield. With his wife and cousin Joan ('the Fair Maid of Kent') he served as his father's representative in Aquitaine, France, where they held court in great style. Returning to England in 1371, he died a week short of his 46th birthday in 1376, probably of dysentery contracted on military campaign years before. He was the first Prince of Wales not to become king, but not before his courage at the battles of Crécy and Poitiers had established him as 'the flower of chivalry' and, as his biographer noted, 'the perfect root of all honour and nobleness, of wisdom, valour and largesse.'

THE HUNDRED YEARS WAR

Between 1337 and 1453, England and France were almost continually at war as a result of two dynastic wrangles. The first dated back to 1066, when William the Conqueror had become King of England while retaining his title of Duke of Normandy. Later English kings also inherited both titles and, as dukes of Normandy, were expected to pay homage to the King of France.

In 1328 Charles IV of France died without a male heir and his title passed to a distant male relative. However, the English King

Edward III maintained that his mother Isabella, as Charles IV's sister and therefore a closer relative, should have had the title. She had been passed over because under French law the crown could not descend through the female line. In 1337 Edward announced that he himself was the rightful King of France, through his mother's lineage, and he refused to pay the customary tribute to Philip VI. Philip immediately confiscated Edward's lands in the French county of Aquitaine, inciting Edward to declare war. In June 1340 the English fleet sailed for France, beginning a conflict which raged on and off throughout the next century.

Most of the actual fighting took place on French soil but the cost of the long drawn-out conflict made the war deeply unpopular in England. In France the consequences were far worse, as the fighting gave rise to general lawlessness, with bands of mercenaries marauding unchecked over the country.

> '… all went ill with the kingdom and the State was undone. Thieves and robbers rose up everywhere in the land. The Nobles despised and hated all others and took no thought for usefulness and profit of lord and men. They subjected and despoiled the peasants and the men of the villages. In no wise did they defend their country from its enemies; rather did they trample it underfoot, robbing and pillaging the peasants' goods …'
>
> From the Chronicles of Jean de Venette

The English were not particularly sympathetic to French suffering. During the century of conflict, English victories at Poitiers, Crécy and Agincourt had been hailed as triumphs and become the stuff

*Warfare was a brutal business that spared neither soldiers nor
innocent townsfolk who were unlucky enough to be caught up in
a siege. Many were subjected to terrible public punishment as an
example to others of the folly of resistance.*

of legend, told over in ballads and chronicles. Military heroes, in
particular the Black Prince and Henry V, were enshrined in English
mythology alongside King Arthur and Brutus, the legendary founder
of Britain.

The Hundred Years War was important for several reasons.
First, it saw the beginning of an alliance between France and

Scotland, which stated that the French and the Scots would support each other in the event of either country being invaded by England. This became known as 'the Auld Alliance' and would be a thorn in the side of English monarchs for years to come. Second, the very nature of warfare changed with the introduction of more modern weaponry, particularly the longbow, and lightly armoured dragoons took the place of heavy cavalry and hand-to-hand sword fighting. Another result of the century of war was a growing sense of nationalism in both the French and the English – and a deep rivalry between them.

EUROPE IN THE TUDOR ERA

The map of Europe in the Tudor period was very different from the one we are used to today. Countries like France and Italy were not unified entities but loose conglomerations of provinces or city-states ruled by powerful dynasties. As a consequence, there were endless disputes at internal levels, as well as those generated by the shifting alliances brokered by their rulers. States changed sides and severed alliances with bewildering rapidity and for reasons that ranged from religious affinity through territorial land-grabs to the avenging of perceived insults to a family member in some dynastic marriage settlement. The opportunities for going to war either against or in support of some other state were manifold.

Traditionally, England's enemies were her closest neighbours: France, just across the Channel, and Scotland, that troublesome wild country at England's northern border. With thoughts of his childhood heroes Henry V and the Black Prince in his head, Henry looked to France first as a chance to prove himself, and it wasn't long before an opportunity arose to pick a quarrel with King Louis XII.

Henry had originally set out to renew his father's friendship with Louis, but then signed a contradictory pact with his own father-in-law, Ferdinand of Spain. Then, in 1511, he took England into Pope Julius II's Holy League, setting himself firmly against Louis and on course for an invasion of France. At this period the papacy combined both spiritual and temporal authority, heading the armies of the papal states.

The Holy League

Between 1508 and 1516, northern Italy was wracked by continual skirmishes in what was known as the War of the League of Cambrai, or the War of the Holy League, primarily between the papal states, the republic of Venice and France. At various points, however, almost every major power in Europe was also drawn into these wars. Pope Julius II, anxious to limit Venetian power, created the League of Cambrai, an alliance binding France, the Holy Roman Empire and Spain to the papal states. Although initially successful, the alliance collapsed owing to friction between the pope and King Louis, at which point Venice and the papal states became allies against France. Louis maintained a strong presence in Italy, and by June 1511, much of northern Italy was in French hands, with the papal army powerless to prevent further advances. In desperation, Pope Julius proclaimed the Holy League, an alliance that included Spain, England and the Holy Roman Empire.

Henry joined the League in 1511 ostensibly in support of the beleaguered papal forces, but clearly with expansionist intentions and the reconquering of his own French territories uppermost in his mind. The military objective was to win back Normandy, in northern France, and Aquitaine in the southwest, ancestral lands that had once

belonged to England but had been lost during the previous century. This was very much against the advice of the royal council, who were more in favour of continuing the old king's methods of slow diplomacy than in risking outright war, but eventually parliament voted the king funds to support an invasion of France and in April 1512 Henry declared war.

It would be another year, however, before English troops arrived in northern France, and when they did it was without the king. An earlier plan for a joint Anglo-Spanish invasion of Aquitaine had ignominiously come to nothing, largely owing to Ferdinand's inadequate support, so it was not until June 1513 that an English fleet of 300 ships landed at Calais. The troops marched through northern France to lay siege to the town of Thérouanne. For six weeks there appeared to be stalemate, but when more troops arrived to relieve the original forces, led this time by a gloriously equipped Henry, everything changed.

At Guinegate on 16 August Henry's mighty forces of cavalry, artillery, infantry and longbowmen scored a stunning victory over French forces still largely composed of foot soldiers armed with pikes. The French forces retreated in disarray. Back in England, the conflict became mockingly known as the 'Battle of the Spurs', thanks to the speed with which the French fled from the field. Henry, no doubt disappointed not to have been allowed to lead the initial charge, took an enthusiastic part in chasing the retreating forces. With this decisive battle, the town of Thérouanne fell to Henry and a few weeks later, after an eight-day siege, the English captured the far more valuable prize of Tournai.

Writing to Maximilian Sforza, Duke of Milan, to inform him of his victories at Thérouanne and Tournai (and writing of himself

in the third person, as was then customary) Henry displayed a characteristic lack of modesty: 'from the time he entered France he has always had the better of his enemies, of whom he has captured many of the noblest.' Henry's first proper foray into France had been successful. He returned to England as much of a hero as he might have wished although, as he soon discovered, he was not the only one to have covered himself in glory.

The Battle of the Spurs was an easy victory for the English and perhaps gave Henry a false impression of future success in France. The king himself reported how his forces had 'advanced straight against the French, causing the artillery to be fired at them, whereupon they immediately began to retire, and were pursued for 10 leagues without great loss to the English.'

NORTH OF THE BORDER

While Henry was engaged with his French campaign, Katherine was left at home as regent. Sensing vulnerability, the Scottish King James IV saw an opportunity to fulfil his part of the Auld Alliance with France. In the hope of diverting troops from being sent to boost the French campaign, he declared war on England. An exchange of increasingly threatening letters between James and Henry was in vain, and back home, in August, Queen Katherine issued an order for the seizure of the property of all Scots living in England. Thomas Howard was ordered to raise an army, and Queen Katherine herself made a rousing speech to the troops, reminding them that 'English courage excelled that of all other nations'. On 3 September, James's army invaded Northumberland, and on 9 September it met with English forces near the village of Branxton, at a location known as Flodden Field.

Raising an army

As there was no standing army in England during the first half of the 16th century, it was the responsibility of the nobility to raise armies from their tenants and workers, to arm them with whatever weapons could be mustered and to command them in the field. Success in battle brought its own rewards, usually in the form of ennoblement for the middle classes or promotion to a higher degree of nobility for those who already had a title. It was the key to advancement in Tudor society. Henry showed his gratitude to Thomas Howard, who led the English forces at Flodden, by restoring him to his dukedom of Norfolk. This had been forfeited by his father during the Wars of the Roses for supporting Richard III. The Howards were to become one of the most powerful families of England and would be major figures in Henry's later life.

The Battle of Flodden

Flodden has been described as the last great medieval battle to be fought in the British Isles, and perhaps it was King James's honourable adherence to the old laws of chivalry that was to prove his downfall. First, he had given the traditional month's notice of his intention to invade, which allowed Katherine time to raise an army and get it into position. Second, he refused an opportunity to attack the English forces when they were in a vulnerable position crossing a bridge as they headed to the battleground. The Scots were also less advanced – or less cunning – than the English in modern warfare. They placed their officers in the front line along with the men, according to the medieval pattern, but this made them too good a target. When the officers were killed, the troops were left with no one to coordinate retreat or regrouping.

Finally, the Scots held a superior position on a hillside, but instead of holding this position, they moved down the hill to engage with the English on what turned out to be marshy ground. Whatever the circumstances, as Raphael Holinshed noted in his Chronicle, 'the battle was cruel, none spared other, and the King himself fought valiantly.' In three hours of fighting, the Scottish army was routed. King James, who had led the troops himself, was killed and his body taken to Berwick-upon-Tweed, the last British monarch to die in battle. It was a disaster for the Scots, who in a single day had lost not only their king, but most of the nobility and a whole generation of young men. It was said that every noble family in Scotland had lost a member at Flodden. The Battle of Flodden was a mortal blow to the Scots, who had initially appeared to have the advantage, with superior cannon power brought down from Edinburgh. This catastrophe put an end to Scottish power for decades.

The Flowers o' the Forest

The lament 'The Flowers o' the Forest' commemorates the nobility of Scotland who died at the Battle of Flodden. The words were set to an ancient Scottish pipe tune sometime in the 17th century, although a version may have existed earlier. Such is the reverence of the Scots for this lament that it is only played at funerals and memorial services.

'I've heard them lilting, at the yowe-milking,
Lassies a-lilting before dawn o' day;
But now they are moaning on ilka green loaning;
The Flowers o' the Forest are a' wede away.

Dool and wae for the order sent oor lads tae the Border!

The English for ance, by guile wan the day,
The Flowers o' the Forest, that fought aye the foremost,
The pride o' oor land lie cauld in the clay.'

For Queen Katherine, however, it was a triumph. She wrote to Henry in France 'it is no need to trouble your Grace herein with long writing; but to my thinking this battle hath been to your Grace and all your realm the greatest honour that could be, and more than ye should win all the crown of France.' She even managed a joke about sending Henry a piece of the King of Scots' coat to trim his banner, and finished with a timely reminder of the involvement of the French in these recent events: 'I send your Grace herein a bill found in a Scottish man's purse of such things as the French King sent to the said King of Scots to make war against you.'

THE FRENCH

Things had begun well for Henry. He had made his mark in Europe and gone some way to establishing England as a major power. But by the end of the year he found himself isolated again when his former allies deserted him and he realized he did not have the resources to go on alone. At this point, guided by the ever-resourceful adviser Thomas Wolsey, Henry pulled off an unexpected diplomatic coup by making peace with King Louis. The deal hinged on an agreement that Henry would be granted an annual pension to represent 'tribute' from his ancestral lands in France, without his actually being acknowledged as their ruler. In a letter to Wolsey, Henry reported that he was to receive 100,000 crowns a year, 'to recompense me for withholding of mine inheritance', but noting also that 'friendship should no longer continue than the payment of money'. Henry was no fool, especially where the French were concerned. He then proceeded to seal the alliance by agreeing to the betrothal of his sister Mary to the elderly Louis. The two were married in October 1514.

It was hardly a suitable match and Mary, well educated and an acknowledged beauty, had little cause to thank her brother. Apart from the huge discrepancy in age – Mary was eighteen, her bridegroom was 52 – Louis was ugly, disfigured by smallpox and already ailing. His previous two marriages had produced no sons and union with the much younger Mary was a last-ditch attempt to do so. Fortunately for Mary, the marriage did not last long: less than three months after the wedding, Louis was dead – worn out, tradition had it, by his efforts to produce an heir. Fortunately, too, those efforts had been to no avail. There were to be no children to keep Mary in France and she was soon back at the English court, although her homecoming was not as joyful as she might have hoped.

Louis' death not only freed Mary from her marriage, it also brought onto the stage Henry's greatest rival, Francis I, the new King of France. As Louis had died without male issue and the law forbade the crown to pass through the female line, he was succeeded by his cousin's son. Tall, athletic, dashing and just twenty years old, Francis was Henry's exact counterpart and harboured the same ambitions. He began his reign with a suitable military flourish by capturing the city-state of Milan in September 1515. This triumph trumped Henry's French victories, but it also helped to focus his mind properly on his glamorous rival. The two men had yet to meet and there must have been a good deal of mutual curiosity between them. Almost exact contemporaries, similar in appearance and much alike in their love of martial arts and ambition for worldly fame, Henry and Francis could either be rivals or powerful allies. Henry chose

In this view of Henry's sister Mary Tudor during her brief reign as Queen of France, the painter has been rather tactful, depicting the 52-year-old King Louis as much younger than his actual age.

the latter, although events dictated that these roles would be reversed many times over the ensuing decades. But before he could take steps to court Francis, international events took another curious turn.

BATTLE OF THE BEARDS

Francis had originally suggested an earlier date for his meeting with Henry, but when Wolsey advised postponing it, Henry, as an assurance of his eagerness, made the rather extravagant promise that he would not shave until they met: 'As a proof of the King's desire, he had resolved to wear his beard till the said meeting. To requite this token of his affection, Francis "laid his hand on his beard, and said surely he would never put it off till he had seen him"'. Francis may have been impressed by Henry's rash offer, but Queen Katherine was not. She begged her husband to shave, but when he refused she made the best of it, putting out a statement that 'Their love is not in the beards but in the hearts.' Eventually Henry gave in and trimmed his beard, earning himself a sharp reproof from Francis's mother, who felt her son had been slighted. This time it was Sir Thomas Boleyn who had the responsibility of pouring diplomatic oil on troubled waters.

Portraits of Henry VIII usually show him with a beard. Tradition has it that Henry first grew a beard after seeing a picture of his rival Francis I with a luxurious growth of facial hair (see page 57), but this is probably apocryphal as portraits from the 1520s show Henry already cultivating a small beard. Naturally, courtiers began to emulate the king's style and allowed their beards to grow, some taking this to excess.

> Throughout his life Henry's style varied little, his beard being neatly close-cropped. Curiously, in 1535 he introduced the novel idea of a beard tax, a graduated levy that varied according to the wearer's social position.

Pope Leo X put forward plans for a general declaration of peace between all the major European states, with the intention of presenting a united Christian front against the threat being posed by the Ottoman Empire to the east. Thomas Wolsey saw an opportunity for Henry to move into the spotlight as a peacemaker, and under the blanket of this general agreement, he brokered an individual treaty of non-aggression between Henry and Francis. Under the terms of the Treaty of London, signed by the two monarchs in October 1518, Francis was allowed to buy back the recently captured Tournai and honour was temporarily restored. Wolsey's stage management of the process ensured that Henry appeared to have been both instrumental in the deal and personally magnanimous towards England's old enemy. But signatures on a treaty were not enough: here was an opportunity for a far more glorious demonstration of brotherly unity to be seen on the world stage. Wolsey set about organizing an event that would bring the two young men face to face, and it would be an occasion more splendid than anything Europe had yet seen.

Charles V, meanwhile, hearing rumours of the proposed meeting and anxious not to be left out of any major diplomacy, arrived in England in 1520 to meet Henry and thank him for his support in his election as Holy Roman Emperor the previous year. Despite having been a candidate himself, Henry had supported Charles largely to thwart the hopes of Francis, who had also been in the running.

Although he was happy to court Francis to suit his own ends, he certainly did not want to see him elevated to so mighty a position. The balance of power had to be maintained. There was a family connection, too, as Katherine of Aragon was Charles's aunt, and during the visit she urged her husband to consider a closer alliance with Charles. The scene was being set for a three-way rivalry of alpha males that would dominate the next decades.

THE FIELD OF CLOTH OF GOLD

The most glittering event Europe had ever seen took place between 7 and 24 June 1520. The location was carefully chosen, on neutral ground just outside Calais, where English and French territories bordered each other.

The whole event was stage-managed with the utmost attention to diplomacy – even the valley was landscaped so that both parties stood at an equal height – and no expense was spared. The setting was a work of art: to accommodate the two monarchs and their enormous retinues, Wolsey built an entire temporary city. The name 'Field of Cloth of Gold' gives some idea of its splendour. Cloth of gold was a fine fabric woven from silk and gold thread that sparkled and shone in sunshine or candlelight. Here it was used extravagantly not only for clothing but also for decorative hangings and for the tented pavilions which housed the major protagonists in the drama. For Henry's accommodation, a temporary palace covering some 10,000 square metres was erected around a central courtyard. The walls, ten metres tall, were built of brick to a height of two metres, with the upper parts made of canvas on timber frames, painted to look like brick. As befitted two military princes, all the decorative imagery was of martial heroes and warlike iconography.

'... in the fenesters, and windows, were images resembling men of warre redie to cast great stones: also the same gate or Tower was set with compassed images of ancient Princes, as Hercules, Alexander and other, by entrayled worke, richly limned with gold and Albyn colours ... for the sundrie countenances of every image that their appeared, some shooting, some casting, some ready to strike, and firing of gonnes, which shewed very honourably.'

Grafton's Chronicle, or Chronicle at Large

The roof, made of oiled cloth, was painted to resemble slates and there were so many tall, glass-filled windows that guests felt as though they were sitting in the open air. The interior of the palace was sumptuous, hung with tapestries and decorated with jewels and golden ornaments, while outside in the courtyard, red wine flowed from two fountains. All this, of course, had to be transported from London in a huge wagon-train of carts and carriages.

Tented pavilions, made of canvas covered with cloth of gold and painted with Tudor livery badges, covered the valley and the ground between was spread with embroidered carpets, giving the impression of a wildflower meadow. In the fields beyond, nearly 3,000 tents housed minor officials and less distinguished visitors. In the French sunshine it looked magnificent. Chroniclers described it as the eighth wonder of the world: it was also a miracle of deception, a fairytale city. Amid all this worldly splendour, religion was not forgotten. There was a chapel, with 35 priests and a choir supplied by the French Chapel Royal, which was acknowledged as one of the finest in Europe.

THE MEETING

Landing at Calais with a train of some 6,000 followers, Henry took up residence at the castle of Guînes, while Francis was lodged at nearby Ardres. On 7 June, after Wolsey and an impressive retinue had paid a preliminary visit to the French party, the scene was set for the meeting of the two monarchs. At the signal from a cannon, the two kings approached each other on horseback, clad in full knightly regalia. They embraced three times, dismounted and embraced again before retiring to their golden pavilion. The actual meeting may have been something of an anti-climax after all the surrounding ceremony, and very little of any importance seems to have been achieved, other than a general commitment to peace. But the personal rapprochement had been made. Henry had looked his great rival in the eye, and each had surely made a rapid assessment of the other's power and magnificence. Wolsey's efforts had not been in vain. The historic meeting between Henry and Francis was portrayed by artists of the day on both sides of the Channel to illustrate the hope that it would usher in a new age of peace and comradeship. Unfortunately, like so many such 'summit meetings', it did not live up to expectations.

And after the meeting came the festivities. The next fortnight was a continual round of feasting, music, masked balls and pageants in which the kings, their queens and all their retinue dressed up. Everyone was in holiday mood. Henry had been sent two monkeys by Sultan Selim I and these provided much entertainment during the feasting, as Cardinal Wolsey recalled: 'The French King was overcome with much curiosity playing with those little knaves that did all they could to steal and pester his advisers, yet he willed them to be present at every banquet.' Records from the royal kitchens show that 2,000 sheep were consumed, along with 40,000 gallons of wine and 14,000

gallons of beer and ale. But the main entertainment, as was to be expected, was sport.

Both Henry and Francis took part in the tilting and jousting, each breaking several lances. Although most of the action was carefully scripted to avoid either injury or loss of face, Henry went too far when, against protocol, he challenged Francis to a wrestling match. The royal pride was dented when he was thrown but it may have been restored when Francis, at some point in the jousting, got a black eye. The tournament ended with a display of pageantry in which courtiers paraded in the costume of heroes of the past. At the end of the celebrations, Wolsey announced a general pardon for the sins of all present, and the two kings parted, vowing to erect a chapel on the site of their meeting as a sign of their eternal amity and hopes for general peace. The magical city was dismantled and everyone went home. Two years later, England and France were at war again.

Bishop Fisher used the occasion as material for a sermon and although, typically, he ended by showing the hollowness of worldly pleasures when compared to those of the kingdom of heaven, his description shows how successful Wolsey had been in putting Henry firmly on an equal footing with the other two princes: 'Was it not a great thing, within so short a space to see three great princes of this world – I mean the Emperor, and the King our master, and the French king; and each of these three in so great honour, showing their royalty, showing their riches, showing their power, with each of their noblesse appointed and apparelled in rich clothes, in silks, velvets, cloths of gold, and such other precious raiments. ... Such dancings, such harmonies, such dalliance, and so many pleasant pastimes ... so delicate wines, so precious meats, such and so many noble men of arms, so rich and goodly tents, such joustings, such tourneys, and such feats of war.'

WAR AGAIN

In the years following, Europe was rendered inherently unstable by the intractable and ongoing hatred between Francis and Charles. As the Venetian ambassador shrewdly noted, they may have kept up an appearance of friendship and peace but at bottom 'they adapt themselves to circumstances but hate each other very cordially.' Henry was initially happy to be cast in the role of peacemaker but eventually, giving up all attempts to mediate between them, he succumbed to his wife's entreaties and threw his support behind her nephew Charles.

In 1523, English soldiers were again marching through France under the command of the Duke of Suffolk, but this time there were to be no triumphs. Just 50 miles short of Paris, Suffolk was forced to retreat and the campaign ended in failure. His disgruntled troops had come close to mutiny during the many long marches in wintry conditions, as Welshman Elis Gruffydd noted in his Chronicle: 'some of the soldiers said they would tarry there no longer, and that they would go home willy nilly the next day … Against this some of their comrades said that what they were discussing was no less than treason … To this these obstinate senseless men answered that it was no worse being hanged in England than dying of cold in France.' Clearly, the attraction of Henry's obsessive desire for land and glory in France was beginning to pall with his subjects.

Charles, on the other hand, was scoring significant victories in Italy, where he captured not only the city of Milan but, at the Battle of Pavia, Francis I himself. This was a major coup. Henry, delighted at Francis's defeat and hopeful of sharing in his new ally's triumph,

suggested they mount a joint invasion of France, after which Henry would reclaim England's ancestral lands and Charles would take the rest. For reasons that are not clear, however, Charles insulted Henry by refusing this offer and further snubbed him by breaking off his betrothal to Henry's daughter Mary. Hopes of a solo English campaign into France ended when nobles throughout the country, already alarmed by the cost of previous campaigns and then by the massive expense of the Field of Cloth of Gold venture, refused to grant Henry funding.

A furious Henry responded to Charles' snub with an immediate volte-face, making overtures to the captive Francis and signing a treaty promising to help negotiate his release. In 1526, on Francis' release from captivity, Henry consolidated this with a further binding agreement not to make a separate peace with Charles. The following year Henry and Francis signed the Treaty of Amiens, pledging eternal peace between their two kingdoms. For once the pledge bore fruit: England and France would be at peace for over a decade, and it was a decade in which Henry needed all the support he could get. He was about to embark on his struggles with the pope.

The Amicable Grant

To support his intended French campaign in 1525, Henry went to the country to ask for an exceptional grant of money. This was known as 'the Amicable Grant', but it was to prove an ironic misnomer. The response from the counties was anything but friendly. The nobility and leading gentry, charged with securing contributions from their various regions, reported nothing but opposition and grumbling. Previous forays into France had cost a fortune and resulted in no significant gain of territory: no one wanted to pay for another

venture. The people were tiring of Henry's schemes as rapidly as the footsoldiers on the ground. Eventually Henry gave in, pretending he hadn't realized the extent of the request.

FATHER OF THE NAVY

Henry's reign marks the beginning of England's legendary naval power and Henry himself is often referred to as the founder of the Royal Navy. As an island nation, England's supremacy depended on the strength of her sea-going forces and the vessels that carried them. Sea power was clearly essential for ferrying troops across to Europe and for defending England's coastline, but in the rapidly accelerating race for colonial dominance in the New World, swift, modern vessels would be of crucial importance. For the moment, this rested with Spain and Portugal, but it was a race that would soon involve England as well.

Although Henry's father had begun to lay the foundations of a shipbuilding programme, by the time he died this amounted to only five royal warships.

By the end of Henry VIII's reign, the navy had more than 40 ships. Henry took an active personal interest in ships and navigation and had a significant degree of knowledge. Part of his childhood education had been in learning to read charts and understand navigational instruments, and he threw himself into the business of building a navy with the same degree of enthusiasm he offered to anything which caught his imagination.

As early as 1512 he commissioned a new flagship, the *Harry Grâce à Dieu*, familiarly known as 'Great Harry'. The first four-masted ship to be built in England, and crewed by 300 sailors, it could carry 350 troops and 50 gunners. Henry realized that the nature of warfare

at sea had to change. In the past, sea battles had been fought by large, unwieldy wooden hulks designed to grapple up against enemy vessels to allow soldiers to engage in hand-to-hand fighting. Most of them were essentially merchant ships requisitioned by the king when occasion demanded. The idea of building and a maintaining a whole fleet of light, speedy warships specially designed to attack and pursue the enemy was entirely new.

The first step was to establish new dockyards where all this construction could take place. Obviously this had to be close to water and, as all the ships of the period were built of wood, a handy source of timber was a major consideration. Henry settled on two sites on the banks of the River Thames, at Deptford and Woolwich. These were perfect locations: not only was the Thames the major gateway to London, far more important as a busy thoroughfare than it is now, but much of the surrounding countryside of Kent was thickly forested with trees. Other allied industries, such as rope-making and iron smelting, quickly grew up alongside the docks.

As demand increased, Henry established other naval dockyards along the south and east coasts, at Chatham and Sheerness in Kent and Portsmouth and Plymouth in the west country. By the end of Henry's reign, Chatham had become the main base of the English fleet, with ships over-wintering in the River Medway. Under Queen Elizabeth, it was the centrepiece of the golden age of English naval supremacy, as William Camden noted in his *Britannia*: 'under this bridge the Medway foams and rolls with great violence and rapidity, and presently abating both, forms a dock finished for the finest fleet the sun ever beheld, and ready on a minute's warning, built lately by our most gracious sovereign Elizabeth for the security of her subjects and the terror of her enemies.'

WARSHIPS

The average Tudor warship carried around 20 heavy cannon and 60 lighter ones, which meant it had to be much stronger than previous vessels and the cannon had to be carefully positioned. They were ranged along one side of the ship so that they could all be fired together in a devastating 'broadside', and in order to make the vessel more stable they were fixed low down, near the waterline. Hinged, watertight 'gunports' could be let down to cover the portholes when the cannon were not in use. Although cannon were the main weapon, most ships also had archers on board – longbowmen aboard the English ships who could fire ten arrows in a minute. These warships were the ultimate status symbol of modern monarchy. They were also expensive, which meant that generally their loss was to be avoided. The object was not to sink an enemy vessel but to disable it by bringing down its masts and rigging; then soldiers would scramble on board and take the crew prisoner, for which they were rewarded with 'prize money'.

Henry was able to hand on to his successors such a fine navy because he always kept pace with developments in modern warfare. In the 1530s he had many of his ships, including the *Mary Rose*, rebuilt and armed with heavier guns. Some cannon were now mounted on gun carriages, to enable them to be wheeled around and repositioned at speed. The English naval ships of this second generation were faster and nimbler under sail, paving the way for the galleons that would defeat the Spanish Armada.

Building new warships was exciting, but there was administration to consider, too, and to this end, towards the end of his reign Henry established the Navy Board, the body responsible for the administrative affairs of the navy and its day-to-day running. The

Board, which was independent of the Admiralty, managed the six naval dockyards and dealt with the building and re-fitting of ships and the business of supplying them. The foundations of the Navy Board laid down in Henry's day were so sound that the institution changed hardly at all for the next 100 years.

The *Mary Rose*

Built at Portsmouth between 1509 and 1511, she was a four-masted carrack weighing 600 tons. She led the English fleet in many naval battles, undergoing a major refit in 1536, but after 33 years' service, the *Mary Rose* sank in the Solent on 19 July 1545, while engaged in an attempt to prevent French ships landing on the Isle of Wight. She was overloaded at the time and, after making a sharp turn, tipped suddenly to one side, allowing seawater to flood in through the gunports. Henry watched helplessly from the shore as the ship disappeared beneath the waves in moments with the loss of almost all on board including the captain, Sir George Carew. Only 30 of the 700 crew were rescued. Although attempts were made almost immediately to raise the ship, the *Mary Rose* lay on the seabed for 400 years until archaeologists discovered the wreck in 1967. In 1982 she finally emerged from the sea. The mud in which she lay had preserved not just the timbers but many of the objects on board. This meant the ship proved a vital resource for documenting Tudor naval history.

Henry the Navigator

The 16th century was the great age of mapmaking, and in his later years, Henry took a great interest in maps, navigational instruments and works of cosmology. He welcomed a stream of scientists and

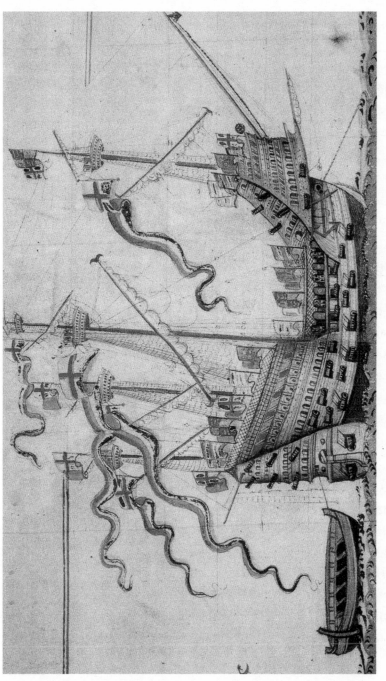

The Mary Rose was Henry's favourite ship, named after his sister Mary. With her height above sea level and the fluttering pennants and flags she seemed almost too delicate and pretty for a warship, but the number of cannon ports proves the opposite. It was, however, these very armaments that would prove her undoing when the sea flooded in through the open ports.

technicians to England, offering them court appointments and royal patronage. Among them, Jean Totz, appointed Royal Hydrographer in 1542, invented a new kind of compass and presented Henry with the latest, state-of-the-art atlas offering what was at the time a complete account of the known world. Another Frenchman, Jean Mallard, presented Henry with a copy of his new book of cosmography. (It turned out to be a hastily revised version of the one he had already presented to Francis I, but Henry made him a court appointment anyway.) All over Europe scientists and mathematicians were engaged in mapping the world, working on ways to calculate distance, the times of sunrise and sunset, the position of heavenly bodies and so on. Presentation copies of their work, usually on vellum and beautifully illuminated, made ideal New Year's gifts for a monarch. Although many of the gifts he received were clearly intended to flatter the king's intellectual image, Henry's thirst for knowledge and his enjoyment of these offerings were genuine. Blessed with a liberal education and with access to the greatest minds in Europe, throughout his life he was fascinated by the new and continually sought to broaden his knowledge, although how much the real experts welcomed his interference is another matter.

DEFENCE OF THE REALM

The second half of Henry's reign saw the beginning of a decline in fortune from the bright flowering of his early days. Between 1538 and 1540, as a result of the king's break with Rome and his desertion by those who had previously been allies, an isolated England was gripped by fears of invasion. In December 1538, the pope issued his bull of excommunication against Henry for the second time and Cardinal Pole was dispatched to rally the Catholic forces of Europe against

Henry. As Francis I and the Emperor Charles were enjoying one of their periods of amity and had recently signed a new peace treaty, the rumours of invasion that swept England were well-founded.

With defence of the realm again a major issue, the populace was put on high alert. The nobles of each county were asked to survey their regions and seek out areas that might be vulnerable to attack, especially those on or near the coast. Thomas Cromwell, writing in February 1539, requested 'expert men of every shire in England being near the sea ... to view all the seacoast where any danger of invasions is likely to be and to certify the said dangers and also best advices for the fortification thereof.' This locally derived information, never gathered before in such detail, was doubly valuable. Not only did it have an immediate use in identifying sites for the line of new defensive forts Henry was planning, it also prompted a flurry of map-making. Never before had England been so carefully described, parish by parish, and working from first-hand observation. This represented a whole new step in the mapping of the realm. It also produced documents of exquisite penmanship, many of which found their way into the royal collection. Henry adored maps, just as he did star charts and other scientific documents, as much for their beauty as for their informational content.

The Device Forts

The string of forts or small castles along the southern coast of England that were created at this time of national crisis is one of Henry's major achievements. Known as the Device Forts, they represented the most serious defence programme known in England since Saxon times. The first phase of building began in 1539 with 30 forts. They were fairly simple in design, mostly consisting of a

central tower surrounded by concentric platforms on which artillery could be placed. Eventually, a line of these forts stretched from Kent across the Downs to Hampshire, ready to repel invasion on this vulnerable part of the English coastline. As he did with naval affairs, Henry took a keen personal interest in the construction and the military engineering techniques relating to the forts, approving and sometimes amending the plans himself.

In the 1540s, a renewed threat from the French initiated a second phase of building, this time around the estuary of the Solent, opposite the Isle of Wight, to protect the vital ports and dockyards at Portsmouth and Southampton. These later forts were more sophisticated in design, more angular in shape with square keeps, and bore traces of Italian architectural style. Calshot, one of the best preserved of Henry's Device Forts or 'Henrician Castles' stands on Calshot Spit, overlooking the Solent. It was built in 1540 to defend Southampton from attack, using stone from nearby Beaulieu Abbey. Unlike many of the second wave of forts, which are square, Calshot was built as a circular blockhouse with a three-storey central keep, most of which survives intact. Pendennis Castle in Cornwall is a good example of the later forts. As the Device Forts were small and manned by relatively small garrisons of around 30 men, it seems unlikely that they were intended to stand alone against a major invasion but were intended more as a first line of defence, functioning as watchtowers around which a larger force could muster.

SCOTLAND – AND A ROUGH WOOING

While England waited nervously for invasion from across the Channel, in the background rumbled the continual threat from the other half of the Auld Alliance. In 1542, irritated by the troublesome

Scots again launching border raids into Northumberland, Henry turned his attention once more to Scotland, now ruled by King James V, his sister Margaret's son. Diplomatic letters to his nephew at first appeared to produce apologies and a willingness to negotiate, but when James failed to appear at a summit conference in York on 18 September, Henry lost patience. He retaliated with border raids of his own but they were hastily organized and met with unexpectedly stiff resistance. The Scots, buoyed up by initial success, were bold enough to risk a major confrontation with Henry's forces.

This was to be a miscalculation. The Battle of Solway Moss on 24 November 1542 resulted, like Flodden 30 years before, in the total humiliation and defeat of the Scottish forces. When the disheartened James V died three weeks later, he left a country in chaos, a hastily convened regency council governing in place of its new monarch Princess Mary, just six days old. Henry, never one to let family feeling get in the way of a good dynastic union, immediately put forward plans for the infant Mary to marry his own son Edward, then almost six. These protracted negotiations for the hand of an infant whose country he had just devastated became known as the 'Rough Wooing'. Although the marriage was initially approved by the Scottish regency, Henry's conditions – particularly the clause that Mary should live in England until the wedding – proved a step too far.

This was one of Henry's biggest mistakes. Had he struck a conclusive military blow against the Scots while they were virtually leaderless and reeling from defeat at Solway, he might have gained control of Scotland once and for all, freeing himself from the threat in the north. As it was, he resorted to diplomacy. Months were wasted while the marriage negotiations went backwards and forwards, giving the Scots time to regroup. When, in the end, the regency council

rejected his plan and cancelled the marriage treaty, he was left with no option but to make a show of force. But with most of his forces by then occupied in France he could only launch a series of punitive raids across the border, attacking and burning the city of Edinburgh. This served to strengthen Scottish opposition: they cancelled all existing treaties with England and allied themselves firmly with Francis I. It appeared that Henry had seriously underestimated the Scots.

MARY, QUEEN OF SCOTS

Mary was the only surviving legitimate child of James V. Six days old when her father died, she was crowned Queen of Scotland nine months later. She spent most of her childhood in France at the court of Francis I and eventually married his grandson Francis II, bringing Scotland and France into even closer union. However, when Francis died just eighteen months after their marriage, Mary returned to Scotland to ascend the throne in her own right. Her second husband and cousin, Lord Darnley, died in mysterious circumstances. When Mary then married the Earl of Bothwell, suspected of having been implicated in Darnley's murder, an uprising forced the queen into imprisonment; she was then forced to abdicate in favour of her son by Darnley, one-year-old James. Mary eventually fled to England and the protection of her cousin Elizabeth but, as many English Catholics considered Mary to be the true heir to the English throne, Elizabeth could not risk her being left at large. Mary spent eighteen years imprisoned in various castles until she was finally found guilty of plotting to assassinate Elizabeth and executed in 1587 at the age of 44.

Mary, Queen of Scots was destined for tragedy from the day of her birth. King James V told on his deathbed, that his wife had given birth to a daughter, sighed 'it cam' wi' a lass, it'll gang (pass) wi' a lass' predicting – wrongly, as it turned out – the end of his own dynasty, the House of Stewart, which had begun with Margerie, the daughter of Robert the Bruce. Like many prominent women of the Tudor period, Mary was cleverly manipulated by powerful men, although her own headstrong nature accounted for some of her misfortunes.

FRANCE AGAIN

Since Henry's first ebullient forays into France in the early years of the reign, England and France had maintained an uneasy peace, but this did not mean that Henry's ambitions in that country were in any way diminished. By 1543 he was once again preparing for war. The merry-go-round of international politics had brought a renewal of hostilities between Francis and Charles V, and England was now allied with the emperor. Together they planned a new incursion into French territory and in June 1544 a force of 38,000 men arrived in France, to be joined a few weeks later by the king himself. However, instead of marching on Paris as agreed, Henry headed for Boulogne. The city fell to them on 18 September, but Henry's triumph was to be short-lived: just a few days later came news that Charles and Francis had signed a peace treaty. Once again, an English attempt to win back her French lands appeared to have been sabotaged by her allies. Henry retreated to England to lick his wounds.

Another invasion

But that was not the end of the story. The French were now determined on revenge, and in 1544 England was again swept by rumours of invasion. Henry hurriedly embarked on the second generation of Device Forts. A French fleet set sail and managed to land troops on the Isle of Wight and the Sussex coast, burning Brighton, but the majority of the French ships were beaten back by bad weather before they came within sight of the English fleet. In minor skirmishes, the only loss was that of Henry's flagship, the *Mary Rose*. England breathed again, but the cost of the French campaign, plus the cost of building the defensive forts, had been enormous. Boulogne, too, proved expensive to maintain, but pride would not allow Henry to cede it back to France. A further ruinously expensive French adventure had achieved virtually nothing. As another peace treaty was signed, parliament was growing impatient with the king.

Between 1542 and 1547, Henry had spent the equivalent of two million pounds in today's money. The parlous state of the royal finances forced him to desperate measures. Crown lands were sold off and, even worse, the royal mint was commanded to debase the coinage by mixing base metal with silver. This was a doubly foolish move, since not only did the resulting inflation cause severe hardship throughout the country but business was affected, too, as other countries became wary of trade with England.

PACIFYING WALES AND IRELAND

Neither Wales nor Ireland had ever caused Henry as much trouble as Scotland, but nevertheless these were two outlying regions with which he was forced at some point to engage.

Henry VIII wore this tonlet (skirted) armour to joust at the Field of Cloth of Gold in June 1520. It was a late replacement for the armour the king had planned to wear and was hastily put together from several older pieces in the royal armouries and decorated by the foreign craftsmen Henry had brought to work at Southwark and Greenwich.

The Welsh, subjugated by Edward I in the 13th century, had caused England few problems since then, but by the 1530s the monarch felt that measures should be taken to incorporate the region more firmly into England. This was fairly simply achieved. A statute of 1536 made English the only language to be used in courts of law in Wales and in the administration of the Welsh counties. The final integration was achieved by the Act of Union of 1543, after which Wales came entirely under English law.

Ireland, though, was more complicated. English concerns there were limited to the region known as the Pale, four small counties around Dublin. Beyond this area, Ireland was a clan-based society where ancient families were permitted autonomy under royal decree but owed no binding loyalty to the English crown. Any measures passed by its parliament's houses of lords and commons had to be ratified by London and ultimate power lay with the Lord Deputy, appointed by the English king. Henry VII had been content with this state of affairs and his son had seen no reason to challenge it until his break with the church brought events into sharper focus.

Ireland was strongly Catholic and had ties with other European co-religionists, especially Spain. The potential for trouble was clear. In 1534 a rebellion sparked by the death in the Tower of the Earl of Kildare brought Ireland under the scrutiny of Thomas Cromwell, who began moves to bring the Pale more firmly under control. Troops were stationed there permanently and 42 statutes, the most important of which confirmed Henry's supremacy over the church, were passed by the Irish parliament. The native Irish lords were persuaded to cede their land to the crown with the guarantee that it would be returned to them under the terms of English law, along with newly created titles that could be handed on through inheritance just as they were in England. Crucially, these native lords would also be permitted to sit in both houses of the Irish parliament, from which they had previously been barred. This was a highly successful piece of diplomacy. As the Lord Deputy of Ireland remarked, 'Titles and a little act of civility weigh more with those rude fellows than a show of force.'

For once Henry had got his way without having to launch the fleet. In 1541 he was declared king of the new Kingdom of Ireland. Persuading the rest of the country to accept an English king, however, was nothing like so simple and would not be achieved without a good deal of bloodshed. It would occupy English monarchs for most of the next century.

CHAPTER FOUR

LIFE AT COURT

The early years of Henry's reign passed peacefully, at home at least. In the intervals between his military campaigns, Henry threw himself into his private life with his customary enthusiasm.

There was always plenty to do – books to be acquired, buildings to plan, painters to commission, tournaments and masques to organize and, of course, hunting. Life at court was a hectic round of pleasure and the money to pay for it always seemed to come from somewhere. Henry and Katherine of Aragon seemed quite well matched, her more mature outlook tempering her husband's natural impatience and ebullience. Perhaps he really had married her out of affection, as he claimed. Throughout the kingdom the entwined initials 'H' and 'K', along with the family emblems – Henry's Tudor rose and Katherine's personal emblem, the pomegranate (*granada* in Spanish) – appeared on everything from the gateways of buildings to the beautifully tooled bindings of books in the royal library. Both wore jewellery bearing the other's initial. It was an overwhelming show of togetherness.

THE PERFECT WIFE

When Erasmus visited the royal couple in 1520, he was much impressed by the queen, declaring 'Where could one find a wife more keen to equal her admirable spouse?' Certainly Katherine was proving herself the perfect consort, entering into Henry's round of activity, applauding his triumphs in the tiltyard and fussing over his safety and his supply of clean underwear when he went off to war. Intellectually they were well matched, in fact Erasmus had found her education to exceed even that of the king. 'She loved good literature, which she had studied with success since childhood.' Well schooled in law, the classics, religion and genealogy, she also found time for more homely, feminine pursuits.

An excellent needlewoman, skilled in embroidery and lace-making, she would often be found sitting among her waiting-women, embroidering shirts for Henry while enjoying the gossip.

Katherine is credited with introducing to England a kind of embroidery known as blackwork, which was particularly popular in Spain. Executed in black thread on white linen, it gave the appearance of lace and was used to decorate cuffs and collars. Because of this it was known as 'poor man's lace' or, because of its origin, as 'Spanish work'. This kind of decoration became immensely popular in the Elizabethan period when embroidery was at its most sophisticated. Blackwork usually employed linear, geometric images or the regular floral shape of a carnation. Because it was cheaper than real lace, it was often used on children's clothing

Right from her arrival in 1501 as a teenage bride, Katherine had made an impression on the populace. Short, with a round face, fair complexion and rich auburn hair, she was not a stunning beauty but attractive and pleasant. The novelty of her Spanish fashion,

especially the hooped farthingale that gave her skirts their particular shape, was noted and widely copied by the aspiring wives of the aristocracy.

Katherine proved herself a woman of spirit, too. In the interim between the death of Arthur and her marriage to Henry, she had not only railed against the indignity of her treatment by Henry VII but had supported her widowed father by taking upon herself the responsibilities of ambassador for her country. Later, left alone as Henry's regent, she had shown courage as well as initiative in handling the Scottish campaign. She had already been on her way north, pregnant but in full armour, to address the troops when the Battle of Flodden ended the campaign. It's hardly surprising, then, that England had taken Katherine to its heart.

Henry's friends

But Henry also needed his male friends around him. He was naturally gregarious and had a genuine talent for friendship: many of the boys who had been chosen as his companions while he was growing up remained close friends into adulthood and were now ready and eager for positions of authority in the state. They had been rewarded generously for their friendship, either by gifts of money or property, or by advancement at court.

This, however, was a two-way process. In return for his largesse, Henry demanded absolute loyalty and did not expect his decisions or desires to be contradicted in any way. On the occasions when such things happened, Henry's wrath was terrible and his revenge deadly. He had already shown his ruthlessness in dealing with those of his father's old advisers who had opposed him. As many of his own companions were to discover, being the king's man was a dangerous

business: of the few who crossed him, those who managed to keep their heads were banished from favour. And as Francis Bacon was to write: 'The fountain of honour is the king, and the access to

Katherine of Aragon in middle age. The fact that she was so much older than her husband had seemed irrelevant for most of their life together, but as time went on, the difference began to tell.

his person continueth honour in life, and to be banished from his presente is one of the greatest eclipses of honour that can be.'

EVIL MAY DAY

Only one event occurred to disrupt these early years of Henry's reign, but it was a shocking one. The first of May, May Day, was a public holiday usually celebrated with good-humoured revelry, but in 1517 it turned into an ugly riot. A mob of a thousand young men, mostly labourers and apprentices, rampaged through the city of London, destroying property and attacking anyone in their way. They also broke into Newgate prison and freed several men recently imprisoned for attacks on foreigners. The authorities were taken completely by surprise. Sir Thomas More, as Under-Sheriff, came out to remonstrate with the rioters, but although he was temporarily successful in calming them, they refused to return to their homes and rushed on to Leadenhall, the district where the city's many foreign merchants operated. Foreign merchants were looked on with some suspicion because it was believed that they managed to avoid the taxes that hindered local exporters' trade. Houses and shops were attacked and stock looted, in particular the premises of John Meautys, a French merchant and secretary to the king, who was suspected of harbouring unlicensed French wool traders.

The violence, although whipped up by agitators, was fuelled by the general resentment of the thousands of foreigners who, it was felt, were taking jobs from local men. According to Edward Hall's Chronicle, there were so many of them 'that the poor English artificers could scarce get any living', and in popular opinion they 'disdained, mocked and oppressed the Englishmen' and 'set naught by the rulers of the City'. The trouble was only brought to an end

when the Lieutenant of the Tower of London ordered his men to fire on the mob. No one was killed, but there were many injuries and the trail of destruction led right through the city.

There followed three days during which a furious Henry, the wily Cardinal Wolsey and the stunned city authorities shifted blame for the management of this ugly episode and debated how best to present it to the public. On 4 May events came to a dramatic conclusion when 278 men, women and children were paraded through the streets and brought before the mayor, the Duke of Norfolk and the Earl of Surrey. The charge was not riot but high treason, since the attack on foreigners constituted a breach of the king's peace. Thirteen people, including youngsters, were condemned and executed on public gallows specially built along the route of the riot.

A further number were reprieved at the last moment on the intercession of Katherine of Aragon and the king's two sisters. Hanging was the most commonly imposed form of capital punishment. The condemned was carried to the gallows on a horse-drawn cart, which was then led away, leaving the victim to hang until dead. Bodies were often left hanging on the gallows for months as a warning to others. This was a brilliant *coup de théâtre*, but there was more to come. At a grand public ceremony in Westminster Hall, 400 prisoners were led before the king with nooses around their necks, ready for execution.

After a long denunciation by Wolsey of both the rioters and the city authorities, various nobles begged the king for mercy and Henry, in a great show of magnanimity, pronounced a general pardon, whereupon the prisoners threw off their nooses and cheered. Wolsey's clever stage management had ensured a public demonstration of justice and mercy while leaving the populace in no doubt as to the extreme punishment the state would inflict in such circumstances.

HENRY THE CONNOISSEUR OF CULTURE

Despite his agile mind and obvious intellectual abilities, Henry seemed to find the business of running the country something of a bore. He much preferred to leave all that to his ministers, dropping in and out of state affairs as it pleased him and sometimes making unilateral decisions on the spur of the moment. This, coupled with his volatile personality, could lead to conflict, but on the whole the wheels of state functioned well enough during the early years. So while the young men he had elevated got on with the business of politics and administration, Henry was free to indulge his favourite occupations, hunting, building and the arts. The Wars of the Roses had brought cultural and artistic life in England to a virtual standstill. Foreign artists had given up visiting the country and monarchs had been too preoccupied to worry about commissioning artworks. The rest of Europe now far outstripped England in cultural life. Henry set out to remedy this by embarking on an orgy of acquisition and commissioning. Probably his greatest coup was to welcome to England the German-born artist Hans Holbein, who arrived in 1526. Over the subsequent decades, the remarkably gifted and prolific Holbein revolutionized the art of portraiture.

Tudor portraiture

In the days before mass media, painted portraiture was important, but its purpose was often seen as practical rather than artistic. For the sovereign and the nobility, portraiture was the most obvious means of displaying wealth and status, but on a more basic level it was also a way of showing the people of the land just what their king looked like – after all, very few ever actually saw him. Similarly, painted portraits were the only things that could be sent abroad in marriage negotiations to show prospective brides and bridegrooms what was on offer. For obvious reasons they tended to be flattering, and in the case of Henry's fourth wife, Anne of Cleves, this famously led to disaster. Portraits ranged from tiny miniatures, usually intended either as keepsakes or for wearing as jewellery, to large-scale paintings. Mostly half- or occasionally full-length, they featured the sitter dressed in his or her best finery and usually wearing jewellery or carrying objects that had allegorical meaning. Gloves, flowers, animals and insects all bore special significance, indicating status or moral virtue, that would be instantly interpreted by the viewer.

Hans Holbein, the king's painter

Usually known as Holbein the Younger to distinguish him from his father, also a painter, Hans Holbein was born in Augsburg, Germany, but began his artistic career in Basel as a painter of religious murals and designer of books and stained glass. He arrived in England with a recommendation from Erasmus to his humanist colleague Thomas More and soon became part of More's cultural circle. By the 1530s he was under the patronage of Anne Boleyn and Thomas Cromwell and in 1536 became the king's official painter. His brief was to produce not only portraits but also festive decorations, tableware and other precious decorative objects.

Holbein is credited with raising the art of portraiture to new heights. He drew and painted with great precision and with a rare ability to capture the character as well as the likeness of his sitters. While endowing his portraits with layers of often mysterious symbolism that continue to fascinate, he brought a new realism to the presentation of his subjects. It is largely thanks to Holbein that we have such psychological insight into the lives of men and women

who dominated the Tudor court, particularly King Henry himeself, whom Holbein painted many times.

Tapestries

The other pre-eminent artistic achievement of the Tudor period – and seen at the time as far more important artistically – was the tapestry, of which Henry amassed an unrivalled collection. At his death he owned around 2,500 tapestries, varying in size from single images to whole series of panels, each of which might be more than a hundred square metres. The best were made in the Low Countries, of wool and silk interwoven with gold and silver thread; in candlelight they sparkled and shone. Unlike portraits, tapestries were always on show and were thus the most obvious indication of their owner's wealth and good taste. Along with scenes of hunting and hawking, favourite subjects were mostly classical or allegorical. As with his fascination with the Arthurian legends, Henry used these tapestries as a way of associating himself and his family with ancient mythological and religious figures. Wall-hung tapestries served a dual purpose as works of art and, more practically, as draught excluders. 'The Triumphs of Hercules' is one of a series depicting heroes of antiquity commissioned by Henry from a Brussels firm in 1542. Hercules is seen overcoming various wild beasts and monsters, feats of strength with which Henry was only too happy to be associated.

More importantly, after his break with Rome he increasingly acquired or commissioned biblical subjects, thus bolstering his claim to be supreme head of the church in England. Scenes featuring Abraham, David or Joshua standing out against their heathen enemies were particularly suitable in this context. The 'Story of Abraham' series, commissioned for Hampton Court to celebrate the birth of Prince Edward, uses the tale of Abraham and his son Isaac to reflect the father-son relationship. At the same time, by recalling Abraham's covenant with God, it legitimizes Henry's own direct Godgiven sovereignty. A hundred years after Henry's death, when the Royal Collection was audited, this series of tapestries alone was valued at an astonishing £8,260. Given that any one of the large panels could cost as much as a new warship, Henry's lavish expenditure did not go unnoticed by parliament. His international reputation as a connoisseur may have risen by leaps and bounds, but the country's coffers were emptying rapidly.

Passing time with good company

Entertainment was high on the agenda. Musicians and jugglers were constantly passing through the court, and Henry employed at least one permanent jester on his staff.

While parliament worried about the rising debts, the court whiled away time, especially in the long winter evenings, in hearing music, singing and dancing. Traditional instruments like the horn, the harp-like psaltery, drum and recorder were still the staples of Tudor popular music, but new instruments such as the viol (an early kind of violin) and the hautboy (a kind of oboe) introduced a more sophisticated sound. Henry was interested in both watching and taking part in pageants and masques. The latter were dramatic entertainments in which players disguised as allegorical figures acted out romantic tales of chivalry and courtly love in verse. Usually performed at Christmas or after a wedding, they were a less testosterone-fuelled version of the chivalric tournament and, like that display, they spared no expense. Skill and ingenuity went into the exotic costumes, wigs and make-up, the sets – working fountains,

the gilded façades of palaces and castles – and special effects such as thunder, lightning and real rain.

THE COURT JESTER

Henry's jester was called Will Somers. Brought to Greenwich in 1525, he was soon in high favour with the king and their curious relationship lasted to the end of Henry's life. He called the king 'Harry', 'Hal', or 'Uncle', the only person allowed to do so and Will was included in at least three family portraits. A 17th-century biography of the jester recalled his kindness and wit: 'But this Will Summers was of an easie nature, and tractable disposition, who . . . gained not only grace and favour from his Majesty, but a general love of the Nobility; for he was no carry-tale, nor whisperer, nor flattering insinuater, to breed discord and dissension, but an honest plain down-right, that would speak home without halting, and tell the truth of purpose to shame the Devil; so that his plainness mixt with a kind of facetiousness, and tartness with pleasantness made him very acceptable into the companies of all men.' In his later years, when Henry was troubled by a painful leg condition, it was said that only Somers could cheer him up. Court jesters were permitted a familiarity unthinkable to ordinary courtiers and often took great liberties. Even Somers sometimes overstepped the mark. In 1535 the King threatened to kill him with his own hand after Somers, apparently for a dare, had called Queen Anne 'a Ribald' and the Princess Elizabeth 'a bastard'. He survived, however, and remained in office even after Henry's death, entertaining the court of Queen Mary and making his last appearance at the coronation of Elizabeth I.

Will Somers, Henry's jester, wears an ordinary coat, not the parti-coloured outfit jesters are sometimes supposed to have worn. Nor does he have a cap and bells, but he is holding a horn as a symbol of his calling. In the background can be seen other entertainers – stilt walkers, jugglers and children flying kites.

The Assault on Château Vert

This masque took place after supper at Cardinal Wolsey's residence, York Place. The audience was led into a great chamber at the end of which was an elaborate castle with three towers and battlements, all covered in shimmering green foil. Hidden inside, the court musicians played, while on the battlements stood eight court ladies in white satin, each representing one of the female virtues. Beauty was represented by the king's sister Mary, Perseverance was Anne Boleyn and Kindness her sister Mary. Opposite, clad in coats of cloth of gold and blue satin cloaks, stood the eight corresponding male virtues. Alongside Youth, Nobility, Loyalty and so on, Henry himself represented Amorousness. The ladies were guarded by young choristers of the Chapel Royal, representing feminine vices such as Disdain and Jealousy. When Desire begged the ladies to descend, Scorn and Disdain prevented this, provoking the knightly virtues to attack. When they did so, however, it was not with cannonballs but with a rain of fruit and rose petals, after which the ladies were released to dance with their partners.

In 1510, for a Christmas entertainment at Richmond Palace, the setting was 'a hill studded with gold and precious stones, and having on its summit a tree of gold, from which hung roses and pomegranates'. Another featured 'an artificial forest drawn in by a lion and an antelope, the hides of which were richly embroidered with golden ornaments; the animals were harnessed with chains of gold, and on each sat a fair damsel in gay apparel. In the midst of the forest, which was thus introduced, appeared a gilded tower, at the end of which stood a youth, holding in his hands a garland of roses.' Courtiers,

ALL GOODLY SPORT

This song was composed by Henry shortly after his coronation.

'Pastime with good company
I love and shall until I die;
Grudge who will, but none deny,
So God be pleased thus live will I.
For my pastance
Hunt, sing, and dance.
My heart is set:
All goodly sport
For my comfort,
Who shall me let [prevent]?
'Youth must have some dalliance,
Of good or ill some pastance;
Company methinks then best
All thoughts and fancies to digest:
For idleness
Is chief mistress
Of vices all.
Then who can say
But mirth and play
Is best of all?
'Company with honesty
Is virtue vices to flee:
Company is good and ill
But every man hath his free will.
The best ensue,
The worst eschew,

> *My mind shall be:*
>
> *Virtue to use,*
>
> *Vice to refuse,*
>
> *Thus shall I use me.'*

their ladies and sometimes members of the royal family dressed up to play various characters or to join in the dancing that rounded off each play. A particular favourite was *The Assault on Château Vert*, in which Henry himself took part. Tradition has it that it was during this performance, in 1522, that Henry and Anne Boleyn first encountered each other.

HENRY, THE MAN OF PROPERTY

If Henry spent wildly on paintings and tapestries, this was insignificant compared to what went into bricks and mortar. Nothing fired Henry up more than the prospect of building a new palace. No English monarch before or since was responsible for so many wonderful buildings, although relatively little of Henry's legacy remains today. Building was a passion among the great Renaissance families – it was, after all, the most visible outward show of one's power, wealth and personal taste – but with Henry it became a mania, and one that was to bring him close to bankruptcy. The royal family already had access to some 60 palaces, castles and manor houses around the country, as well as a number of residences in and around London, but Henry set about building, renovating and extending with a will. His usual plan was to acquire an existing building and, using this as a nucleus, build around it in the modern style. In this way he transformed the city residences of Whitehall and St James's

Henry's palaces were quite different in character. A drawing of 1562 shows Richmond Palace, with its curious bulbous onion domes on top, erected in 1501 by Henry VII and later altered by his son.

and created a whole chain of country palaces, mainly in the Surrey countryside southeast of London.

Eltham and Richmond

These were the major palaces Henry inherited. Eltham, where he had grown up, remained a favourite family home for celebrating

Christmas and New Year holidays, but was gradually abandoned as too small. Anne Boleyn left her mark on the palace, inserting ten of her badges into the glass of the gallery, and in 1534 both the royal daughters, Elizabeth and Mary, were temporarily lodged there. Richmond Palace, up river from the city, had been built by Henry VII and named in honour of his earlier title, Duke of Richmond.

Bridewell

Bridewell Palace was built on the banks of the Fleet River in the City of London, on the site of the medieval St Bride's Inn, named after a nearby well dedicated to St Bride. A large rambling building set around three courtyards, it cost Henry £39,000 and he was to live there on and off between 1515 and 1523. In 1528 it housed the papal delegation during the debate about the annulment of Henry's marriage to Katherine and after that ceased to function as a royal palace and was leased to the French ambassador. Typically, Henry had either grown bored with it or wanted to free himself of unhappy memories. By 1555 it had become a poorhouse and in the following year a prison, since when the name Bridewell has become a generic term for a jail.

Whitehall

Whitehall Palace, in the very heart of London, was the dream home Henry and Anne Boleyn planned, drawing up the first plans themselves at Christmas 1529. The royal family had lost its main London seat when the Palace of Westminster was partially destroyed by fire in 1512. After this, although Westminster continued to serve as the seat of parliament, it was no longer used as a residence. Around the same time Cardinal Wolsey acquired an adjacent church property called York Place and made it into a magnificent mansion, said to rival any of the king's properties. When Wolsey fell from power in 1530, Henry immediately took possession of York Place and set about vastly extending it. The new building became known as Whitehall Palace, after the white ashlar stone with which it was faced. Built in the typical Tudor style, it looked rather like Hampton Court, with timber framing, oriel windows and gatehouses. Boasting some 1,500 rooms heated by open fireplaces and ceramic stoves, it was one of the biggest palaces in Europe. Predictably, Henry included a sports centre with tennis courts, bowling alley and a tiltyard, all with spectator galleries. The royal suite was on the second floor, directly over the rooms in which ministers conducted affairs of state. This 'privy (private) gallery' was heavily guarded and out of bounds to all but the king's closest companions, but close enough to the seat of power to allow Henry immediate access to events. Whitehall witnessed Henry's marriages to Anne Boleyn and Jane Seymour and he also died there, but it was never his favourite residence, perhaps because it held bad memories of Anne and her betrayal.

St James's

Henry had St James's Palace, second only to Whitehall among the London royal residences, built on the site of a former leper hospital dedicated to St James the Less, from which the palace and its nearby park took their names. It was built between 1531 and 1536 in the typical red-brick Tudor style around four courtyards, its gatehouse topped with turrets with mock battlements. Although Henry hardly lived there, St James's saw several significant events in his lifetime. Anne Boleyn stayed there the night after her coronation and on two of the fireplaces the initials H and A can be seen carved inside a lovers' knot. Two of his children died there: his illegitimate son Henry

Fitzroy and his daughter Mary, whose heart and bowels were buried in the palace's Chapel Royal. Henry's younger daughter Elizabeth I was said to have spent the night there while awaiting the invasion of the Spanish Armada. It remains the official residence of England's sovereign, although none has lived there for almost two centuries, and it gives its name to the royal court, the Court of St James's, to which foreign ambassadors are still formally accredited.

Hampton Court

When Cardinal Wolsey finally fell from power in 1530, his magnificent palace at Hampton Court was confiscated along with all his other goods and properties, and Henry finally got his hands on the place he had long coveted. Some felt, though, that it had been Henry's all along. Certainly it had been largely financed by the gifts he had showered on Wolsey in his glory days and Henry had stayed there whenever he liked. Wolsey had acquired the manor house that formed the nucleus of Hampton Court in 1514, as a measure of Henry's gratitude for his successful managing of the French wars. He set about expanding this modest place into a huge residence, painted and gilded and hung with priceless tapestries and paintings. Henry's plans for Hampton Court were hugely ambitious. He quadrupled the size of the kitchens, and the Great Hall alone took five years to complete. So anxious was Henry for its completion that he had the masons working through the night by candlelight. The great Tudor gateway with its astrological clock (see here) is sometimes known as 'Anne Boleyn's Gate'. But this display of extravagance did not go unnoticed, especially among Wolsey's many enemies. John Skelton, Henry's old tutor and a sharp satirist, wrote 'The king's court should have the excellence/But Hampton Court hath the preeminence'.

After Wolsey's death, Hampton Court became Henry's favourite residence. He went on to build new apartments for himself and his wives, together with pleasure gardens, a hunting park, tennis courts, a bowling alley and even multiple toilets – an unheard of luxury.

Nonsuch

Nonsuch Palace, about five miles from Hampton Court in Surrey, was Henry's showpiece and his attempt to outshine Francis I's spectacular Palace of Fontainebleau, begun earlier in the same year. The name says it all – no such palace had ever been seen before. Nonsuch was the only one of the royal houses to be built from scratch, rather than being a modification of an existing building, and thus represents to a great extent Henry's own vision. The most intriguing of Henry's palaces – because it has so completely disappeared – was Nonsuch. Beautiful and vastly expensive, it was still incomplete when the king died.

To enable Henry to realize his dream of building what would be the first Renaissance palace in England, two Florentine architects were engaged – Antonio di Nunziato d'Antonio, known as Toto, and Bartolommeo Penni. Building began in 1538, on the thirtieth anniversary of the king's accession, and the work was substantially completed by 1541, although work on the extravagant decorative scheme was still in progress when Henry died in 1547. By that time, costs had risen to more than £24,536, half as much again as was spent at the much larger Hampton Court. A whole village and its church were swept away to accommodate the new construction. Often referred to as a hunting lodge, Nonsuch was really a 'privy palace', for the private enjoyment of the king and his inner circle of companions. This accounts for the lavish decoration. It was certainly much

smaller than other houses. Whereas Hampton Court covered six acres, Oatlands ten and Whitehall an astounding 23 acres, Nonsuch covered only two. When the court went there, courtiers had to be put up in tents outside.

The two-storey timber-framed buildings were set around open courtyards. The main gatehouse on the north front had brick and stone turrets built in traditional Tudor style, but the south front had a smaller gatehouse complete with clock, and towers at each end topped by onion-shaped cupolas and weather vanes. The timber framing was faced with slates covered in gold leaf, and the upper floors were covered in white stucco reliefs: shining in the sun, it looked like a real fairytale palace.

It was the decoration, however, that took people's breath away. There were three tiers of reliefs, almost life-size, showing Roman emperors above, gods and goddesses in the middle and classical scenes at the bottom. The centrepiece of the inner courtyard was a relief of Henry himself together with Prince Edward. Most of the reliefs were made by William Kendall and his force of 24 workmen. The king's apartments were on the west side of the inner courtyard, with the queen's apartments on the east, and a long gallery in the connecting south wing. There were formal gardens laid out with classical statues. Tragically, not a trace of this wonderful palace remains. Demolished in 1683, it is known only through a drawing by Georg Hoefnagel (1568).

Oatlands

Henry acquired the medieval moated manor house near Weybridge in Surrey in 1538 and set about extending it into a palace for his fourth wife, Anne of Cleves. Like many of the great houses built after the dissolution of the monasteries, Oatlands was constructed using stone taken from the ruins of a nearby abbey church, in this case Chertsey Abbey. The red-brick palace consisted of three adjoining courtyards, with the usual battlemented gateway.

Woking

The moated manor house near Woking in Surrey was a family property used by Henry's grandmother and his father before he himself began remodelling it between 1515 and 1543. Smaller than many of Henry's building projects, and set among good hunting territory, Woking also had fish ponds and a fine kitchen garden. In 1535, Henry also purchased the nearby manor house of Chobham, which he used as another hunting lodge, extending the grounds to 500 acres. A letter dated September 1514 gives some idea of Henry's activities in the area: 'The King went to Oatlands and there in the meads under Chertsey was killing stags holden in for the purpose, one after another all the afternoon, although they were warned by the trumpets and made known thereby if they did enter any deer of prize ... and on Thursday the King lyted at Byfleet and from there I took my leave and from Oatlands he removes to Chobham or Woking, I know not whether the first and then to Guildford and so on to Windsor.'

Other properties

Henry was also notorious for appropriating properties he coveted from their owners. Some estates were confiscated when their owners fell from grace or were executed, as was the case with Wolsey, others were simply handed over to the king when he expressed a liking for them. Failure to do this would have incurred wrath on a scale that

no one wanted to risk. For example, Thomas Cranmer, Archbishop of Canterbury, owned the beautiful country house of Knole, in Kent, and its surrounding deer park. The great house of Knole was bequeathed to the See of Canterbury on the death of its builder, Archbishop Thomas Bourchier, and eventually came into the hands of Thomas Cranmer. It is reputed to be a 'calendar house', having 365 rooms, 52 staircases, twelve entrances and seven courtyards, although few have managed to count them all. Despite the fact that Cranmer supported Henry throughout his argument with Rome and the following religious reforms, Henry wanted Knole for himself and in 1538 Cranmer found himself with no option but to hand it over.

Many of these places were never lived in by Henry on a permanent basis. Those in the country were mainly used as lodgings when, during the long summer months, virtually the entire court set out on 'progress' or on hunting expeditions. Some properties were handed on to others as rewards for service, others were rented out in an attempt to make much-needed cash. Indeed, during Henry's reign, property became a serious element in the economy. For Henry, though, the enjoyment was in the creation of beautiful buildings. His palaces, including those built as hunting lodges, were filled with exquisite furniture and had fine libraries where even the binding of the books matched the overall decorative scheme.

It's difficult to be sure how much time the king and queen spent in any one place. Henry's natural restlessness prompted him to move around a lot and in the summer it was usual for the whole court to pack up and tour the country to avoid outbreaks of plague. This meant travelling with clothing, furniture, bedlinen and cooking utensils packed into wagons and a huge retinue of courtiers and ladies-in-waiting. Sometimes they stayed in a royal palace, sometimes

they simply descended on a country house whose owner was bound to offer lodgings for as long as it took the king's fancy. Aristocratic families dreaded the potentially bankrupting process this entailed, but refusal was impossible. Even when the king went off to hunt, he was preceded by an army of workmen whose job it was to move the huge 'village' of prefabricated huts and tents that were needed to accommodate his attendants.

CRACKS IN THE MARRIAGE

For fifteen years Henry and Katherine appeared to be content with each other. She had proved herself a loving and supportive wife and had shut her eyes to Henry's occasional indiscretions, although these appear to have been fairly minor for a man in his position at that period. But as the years went by, the difference in their ages began to tell and the shadow of childlessness fell between them. By now Katherine had endured as many as ten pregnancies, all but one of which had ended in tragedy. The strain of suffering so many stillbirths and miscarriages was beginning to show. Her last rec-orded pregnancy, in 1518, had resulted in yet another stillbirth. Katherine was now 40 and past the age where she might be expected to produce an heir. She had put on weight and by 1525 had the appearance of a portly and middle-aged matron. She began to withdraw from the bustle of court life, spending more time in her apartments with the faithful waiting-women who had accompanied her from Spain so long ago. Henry, on the other hand, was in his mid-thirties and, although he was no longer slim and athletic, retained much of his vigour.

The question of a male heir began to preoccupy him more and more. Although Katherine believed that their daughter Mary would be allowed to inherit the throne, Henry did not. England had never

had a queen who ruled in her own right and in his view women were not intended for government. Besides, any Queen of England would almost inevitably marry a foreign prince, who might then attempt to become king rather than consort. He could not risk this threat to the hard-won Tudor succession. He needed a son. But in fact he already had one, albeit illegitimate, born to his mistress of some eight years, Bessie Blount.

In 1519, Bessie gave birth to Henry's illegitimate son. Although Henry acknowledged the child and had him brought up at court as a royal prince, his birth seems to have marked the end of the affair. Bessie was married off to a suitable husband, Gilbert Talboys, who soon obligingly died and left her a widow of comfortable means. Although she disappeared from court, the fact that she had proved Henry's ability to father a son made her something of a celebrity and the saying, 'Bless 'ee, Bessie Blount!' was often heard on the streets of London. Bessie reappeared briefly in royal circles some years later as a lady-in-waiting to Anne of Cleves, Henry's fourth wife, but left the court after that marriage was dissolved and died shortly afterwards, probably of consumption.

A SON AT LAST

Henry's only surviving son was born on 15 June 1519 and was known as Henry Fitzroy. The name 'Fitz-roy' proclaimed to all and sundry that he was the son of the king (*roi* in French) and he was even given his father's forename. Henry made no secret of the boy's existence and even showed him off to visiting ambassadors, no doubt proud that at last he had a son, even if not a legitimate heir. Cardinal Wolsey, who stood as godfather, referred to the boy as 'Your entirely beloved sonne, the Lord Henry Fitzroy'.

BESSIE BLOUNT

Elizabeth Blount was the daughter of Sir John Blount, a loyal but minor servant of the royal family who had accompanied Henry on his French campaign in 1513. Bessie, as she was known, was barely nineteen and a great beauty and it wasn't long after her arrival at court as lady-in-waiting to Katherine of Aragon that she caught the king's eye. Around 1514 she became his mistress, a relationship that was to last for several years and was common knowledge, although Bessie was never recognized as the 'official' royal mistress.

Little Henry was brought up privately in various royal households until the age of six, when the king took the significant step of acknowledging his son more publicly. On 18 June 1525 the boy travelled by barge along the Thames with a retinue of knights and squires to arrive at Bridewell Palace, where in a long and solemn ceremony he knelt before his father to be created first Earl of Nottingham and then Duke of Richmond and Somerset. The ceremony was followed as usual with much feasting and lavish entertainments. The king had done his only son proud. But not everyone was happy. Katherine, no doubt concerned for her nine-year-old daughter Mary's prospects in the light of all this, made her feelings clear.

The Venetian ambassador noted that 'It seems that the Queen resents the earldom and dukedom conferred on the King's natural son and remains dissatisfied. At the instigation it is said of her three Spanish ladies her chief counsellors, so that the King has dismissed

them from court, a strong measure but the Queen was obliged to submit and have patience.'

The king took an interest in the boy's education and upbringing, and the teenage Fitzroy was granted many significant appointments. He became Lord High Admiral of England, then Lord President of the Council of the North and Warden of the Scottish Marches – giving him responsibility for the whole of northern England – and then Lord Lieutenant of Ireland. There was even a plan to crown him king of that country, until fears that the creation of a separate monarch might lead to instability put an end to the idea.

In 1533, at the age of fourteen, Fitzroy was married to Mary, daughter of Thomas Howard, Duke of Norfolk, but their marriage was never consummated, perhaps because Henry was thought to be consumptive.

According to the French ambassador, he was 'a most handsome, urbane and learned young gentleman, very dear to the King on account of his figure, discretion and good manners. ... He is certainly a wonderful lad for his age', while his fellow ambassador from Venice noted 'so much does he resemble his father'.

There is no doubt that the king was both proud and fond of his only son. But in 1536, while legislation was under way to allow him eventually to ascend the throne, Henry Fitzroy suddenly sickened, and on 15 July at St James's Palace, he died. His father-in-law ordered his body to be sealed in lead and taken by coach for secret burial in Framlingham, Norfolk, but instead servants piled the body into a strawcart and the only son of the King of England made his last journey mourned only by two attendants following at a distance.

The arrival of this child in 1519 may have been a source of minor embarrassment but it had proved one thing: Henry was

capable of fathering a healthy male child. He therefore assumed that the explanation for his childless marriage must lie with Katherine. In Henry's mind the old nagging doubt about the morality of his marriage to his dead brother's wife began to surface again. Was the inability to produce an heir God's punishment for flouting His law? Henry began to fret about his marriage. And in the overheated circles of court gossip, rumours of a possible divorce began to circulate.

CHAPTER FIVE

ALL THE KING'S MEN

In the early years of his reign Henry set about establishing his personal power base, rapidly promoting bright young men to positions of influence and showering them with titles. Unlike the later James I, who similarly promoted a whole host of personable young men but for reasons other than their abilities, Henry's policy was without any sexual undertone. He simply liked and admired young men like himself who were skilled in the manly arts, had the necessary attributes of courtesy and education and shared his love of sport and hunting. He liked having friends around him.

THE PRIVY CHAMBER

This most influential department of the royal household – a body quite separate from the Privy Council – was established under Henry VII as an administrative body of gentlemen, ushers, grooms and pages, but under his son it became more like an intimate circle of close friends.

At the top of the hierarchy were the Groom of the Stool and the

Chief Gentleman of the Chamber, and below them a number of other gentlemen who 'dilligently attend upon the king's person … doeing humble, reverent, secrett and lowly service'. In other words, virtually any service, however intimate, that the king might command, and it's important to remember here that the king was hardly ever alone. These gentlemen dressed and undressed him, organized his hunting expeditions, liaised with the nobility over military matters and, most tellingly, kept an eye on everyone else at court.

Mostly well educated, the sons of noblemen or high-ranking gentry, the members of the Privy Chamber also acted as personal secretaries, carrying out a variety of administrative tasks within the king's private rooms. This curious amalgam of civil servant and nursemaid was not considered unusual in an age when bodily functions were performed with less modesty than now and these positions were highly prized. A gentleman received £50 a year, a gentleman usher £30, and a groom £20, plus whatever gifts and bonuses came their way, but the main prize was status. Gentlemen of the Privy Chamber had the ear of the king and often exerted more influence over him than his wife. Over the next few years their number gradually increased as newly ennobled, ambitious young men recognized the advantages of holding a post so close to the king.

Groom of the Stool

Despite its curious name and odd origins, this was an important and much sought-after appointment. It originally meant the person who was responsible for providing the portable toilet, or 'close stool', for the king's use, and for overseeing the washing facilities afterwards. Obviously, whoever carried out this very intimate task spent a lot of time alone with the king and inevitably became his close confidant.

Over time, the title was awarded to the king's closest companions, those who spent time with him in the Privy Chamber, or private apartments. He also managed the privy purse, Henry's personal expenditure. Of Henry's six grooms of the stool, two were eventually beheaded for high treason: Sir Henry Norris in 1536 and Sir Michael Stanhope in 1552.

THE PRIVY COUNCIL

The Privy Council, or King's Council, was a body separate from parliament, composed of the nobility, bishops and various other high-ranking officials whose function was to advise the sovereign on legislation and administrative affairs. It was intended to function by collective responsibility – decisions were taken and warrants signed by all members, and in theory there was no all-powerful minister to dominate proceedings. Since laws made by the king and supported by the Council, rather than on the advice of parliament, were regarded as valid, the Council wielded a good deal of power. However, with the rise of first Wolsey and then Cromwell, this began to change. Both men monopolized affairs of state by arriving at decisions in private with Henry and presenting the Council with a *fait accompli*.

The Star Chamber, created by Henry VII, was essentially a sub-committee of the Privy Council. It could impose penalties for acts which were regarded as immoral but not technically illegal. Its original intention was to cut through red tape and speed up legal proceedings, but it could also be arbitrary and subjective, an instrument of oppression. Later in Henry's reign it became a weapon for bringing actions against anyone who opposed the king's policies. People were encouraged to bring their cases to the Star Chamber rather than to the lower courts, thus ensuring that justice was often

bypassed. Sessions were held in secret, without a jury, and there was no right of appeal.

The Howards

The Howards had been members of the nobility for a hundred years, but over that time they were subject to the fortunes of war. Losing their dukedom of Norfolk by being on the losing side in the Wars of the Roses, they regained it thanks to Thomas Howard's success at the Battle of Flodden. Under Henry VIII they grew in importance to become the most prominent Catholic family in England, their success largely due to the boundless ambition of Thomas, the third duke, and his clever manipulation of the younger members of his family. Thomas Howard, who succeeded his father as third Duke of Norfolk in 1524, had won his spurs on the battlefield, serving with distinction against the Scots and in Ireland, before securing court positions. Loyal service and friendship to the king won him high office but his personal ambitions in the sphere of Henry's personal life brought him within a hair's breadth of disaster. He is portrayed by Holbein in full regalia as Earl Marshal of England and wearing the Order of the Garter.

Thomas scored highly by getting three women married into the royal family, but this triumph was dulled when both his nieces, Anne Boleyn and then Catherine Howard, were executed. He also managed to get his daughter Mary married to Henry's illegitimate son Henry Fitzroy, but this too ended in failure. After Fitzroy's early death, Mary blamed her father for not securing her a better settlement from the king. Having miraculously survived the Catherine Howard episode, Howard once more redeemed himself through war, fighting in France and Scotland, but he was let down

yet again by his offspring. His irresponsible son Henry, Earl of Surrey, made an unauthorized and boastful change to his coat of arms, claiming descent from King Edward the Confessor, and was also heard to brag that his father would be Protector to Prince Edward when Henry died. This was too much for Henry, who had the upstart executed for treason and had his father hauled off to the Tower. The death sentence had been pronounced, but Henry died before it could be carried out, allowing Howard to cheat death yet again. As it was, his vast estates were seized and he spent the whole of the reign of Edward VI in the Tower before being released by Queen Mary and restored to some of his lands.

The Boleyns

Thomas Boleyn was married to Lady Elizabeth Howard, sister of Thomas Howard, the third Duke of Norfolk, and it was this connection that eased him into a successful diplomatic career under Henry VII. The Boleyns were not exactly *nouveau riche*, but they had originally made their money in trade and were thus looked down on by the true aristocracy, despite Boleyn's position at court. Hever Castle, home of the Boleyn family, had been purchased by Thomas Boleyn's grandfather, a wealthy cloth merchant, and the family was always slightly tainted by associations with trade. Despite this, Boleyn was created Knight of the Garter in 1523.

By 1529, having by then ushered both his daughters into the king's bed, Thomas was Earl of Wiltshire and of Ormond, with a family base at Hever Castle in Kent. But the luck of the Boleyns ran out spectacularly with the executions of both Anne and her brother George in 1536, and of George's wife Jane in 1542 along with her mistress Catherine Howard. Neither of the elderly parents survived

these blows for long, Thomas dying in 1539 and his wife in 1538. In the end, however, the Boleyns had the last laugh: it was their granddaughter Elizabeth who would eventually succeed to the throne to become England's most renowned monarch.

The Seymours

The Seymours traced their origins back to the Normans but although they had advanced through judicious marriages to fairly high standing in their local county of Wiltshire, they were of no particular interest until the reign of Henry VIII. Sir John Seymour, having come to Henry's notice by quashing a rebellion in Cornwall, then attended him at the Field of Cloth of Gold and during the visit of Charles V in 1522, becoming a trusted adviser. It was at the Seymours' family manor house of Wolf Hall that Henry is reputed to have first noticed the family's eldest daughter, Jane.

When Henry married Jane he elevated her brother Edward to a position of some power as Earl of Hertford and even after her death, perhaps out of love for her, he continued to favour the family. But it was not long before the Seymours, as representatives of the new reforming religion, were locked into a power struggle with the Catholic Howards, father and son, that only ended with the execution of Henry Howard and the imprisonment of his father. The future then looked bright for the Seymours, who seized every opportunity. After the king's death, Edward Seymour became Lord Protector, ruling the country during the infancy of his nephew Edward VI, while his brother Thomas married the king's widow Katherine Parr. But fate eventually caught up with them too. There was friction between the brothers and in 1549 Thomas was accused of plotting to seduce Princess Elizabeth and beheaded. In

1552 his brother Edward followed him to the block, charged with mismanaging the Protectorship, although many felt it was his arrogance and ambition that had really brought him down.

THE NOBILITY

There were around 50 noble families in England, while around 2,000 families belonged to the aspiring gentry class, and Henry's generosity in bestowing titles was an astute way of getting these 'new' men on his side. This would become even more important when he became embroiled in dispute with the church. During his dispute with the pope he greatly increased the numbers of the secular nobility to enable them to outnumber the religious lords, creating seven new barons and advancing three secular peers in 1529 alone.

COMMITMENT AND TACT

Being a member of the Privy Chamber meant 24-hour commitment to the king's business and a good deal of tact.

'It is ordeyned that such persons as be appointed of the privy Chamber, shall be loving together, and of good Unity and accord keeping secrett all such things as shal be done or said in the same, without disclosing any part thereof to any person Not being for the time present in the said chamber, and that the King being absent, without they be commanded to goe with his Grace, they shall not only give their continuall and diligent attendance in the said Chamber, but also leave hearkening and inquiring where the King is or goeth, be it early or late, without

grudgeing, mumbling, or talking of the King's Pastime; late or early going to bedd.'

The Ordinances of Eltham, 1526

FROM GENTRY TO DUKEDOM

Rising from East Anglian gentry family to a dukedom in just five years, Charles Brandon is the best example of the advancement available through Henry's patronage. Brandon's father had been Henry VII's standard-bearer at the Battle of Bosworth and had died defending the king who, to show his gratitude, had Brandon's son brought to court as a playmate first for Prince Arthur and then for Henry. Thanks to the friendship begun in their boyhood, Brandon was one of very few men who managed to retain the king's good favour throughout his life, although their friendship was at times severely tested. Handsome, brave and charming, Brandon was adored by women and admired by men in equal measure. He was also Henry's principle jousting companion: the only man who could withstand the king's energetic forays.

After distinguishing himself at the sieges of Thérouanne and Tournai in 1513, Brandon was rewarded with the dukedom of Suffolk but, in spite of this, he almost lost the king's favour in 1515 when, sent to escort the newly widowed Mary, the king's sister, home from France, he secretly married her. (Brandon's personal affairs were somewhat tangled as he had been married twice before, first to Margaret Neville and then to Anne Browne. Anne had died in 1511 but Margaret was still alive, their marriage having been annulled on the grounds of consanguinity. Brandon had to obtain a papal bull to assure the validity of his marriage to Mary.) Henry, who had been promoting a quite different and politically useful match between Brandon and Margaret of Savoy, was furious. He demanded the return of all Mary's plate and jewels, plus the whole of her dowry from the French king.

Brandon was in no doubt as to the dire straits his marriage had got him into. Not only had he incurred Henry's wrath, his rapid rise to power had won him many enemies who were busily inflaming the king against him and he feared seriously for his life. On 5 March 1515 he wrote to Wolsey, then Archbishop of York, in some desperation:

> 'And so, to be plain with you, I have married her heartily …
> My lord, I am not in a little sorrow if the King should know it,
> and that his Grace should be displeased with me. For I assure
> you that I had rather have died than he should be miscontent
> … Let me not be undone now, the which I fear me shall be,
> without the only help of you. My lord, think not that ever you
> shall make any friend that shall be more obliged to you … for
> I assure you that I have as heavy a heart as any man living,
> and shall have till I may hear good tidings from you.'

Wolsey duly intervened on the couple's behalf and won the king over, arranging a second marriage at Greenwich. Brandon's story illustrates the extent to which the political and the personal were intertwined. No doubt Henry was genuinely hurt by the deception of 'the man in all the world he loved and trusted best', but it's equally possible that this was an opportunity for the king to get his hands on a useful haul of treasure to boost his rapidly emptying coffers. Whatever the reason, the pair were banished from court to live quietly in the country for a few years until Henry eventually relented; by 1520

Brandon was back at the king's side at the Field of Cloth of Gold. After the fall of Wolsey, Brandon's power increased enormously. He was entrusted with overseeing most of the great events, acting as High Steward at Anne Boleyn's coronation and carrying out the dismissal of Katherine of Aragon's household, a task he found much against his nature. When his wife Mary died in 1533, Brandon married his ward, Catherine Willoughby. She was just thirteen and betrothed to his son, but as the boy was considered too young to marry, the ever-resourceful Brandon married her himself in order to secure her dowry lands. When Brandon died in 1545, the king paid for his old friend's burial in St George's Chapel, Windsor.

THE SELF-MADE MEN

For Henry, the ideal minister would be one who was smart enough to take over the business of government but who was free from the taint of family ambition. Perhaps it's not surprising, then, that of all his political advisers, the two on whom he depended most were not drawn from the nobility, but were self-made men from obscure origins. They were Thomas Wolsey and Thomas Cromwell.

Thomas Wolsey

Wolsey was one of the few men from his father's regime who Henry was glad to keep on in his own service. Born the son of a butcher in Ipswich, East Anglia, Wolsey had studied at Oxford before being ordained a priest in 1498. After holding various church livings he entered the service of Henry VII as royal chaplain and secretary to one of Henry's chief advisers, and it was here that his remarkable organizational abilities and willingness to take on tedious administrative tasks were noted. The young Henry VIII, realizing the

*Thomas, Cardinal Wolsey in front of a window through which can be seen
Cardinal – now Christ Church – College, Oxford, which he founded.*

extent of the paperwork and dull administrative detail involved in kingship, was only too happy to hand it over to this assiduous and seemingly tireless workhorse.

A rather unlikely personal rapport developed between the king and the butcher's son. Behind Wolsey's capacity for apparently dull work lay a brilliant mind and Henry must have recognized in his adviser a lively intelligence and modernizing ambition that matched his own. By 1509 Wolsey had the post of Almoner, in charge of a large proportion of the royal funds, and a seat on the Privy Council. In this context, he was one of the few who supported Henry's decision to go to war in France and when those counsellors who had opposed the war were toppled from power, Wolsey became Henry's most trusted adviser. By the end of 1515 he was Lord Chancellor.

Wolsey was soon indispensable to Henry. After all, it was largely thanks to him that the king was able to indulge his life of pleasure. While Henry dashed around the country on hunting expeditions, he could be sure that faithful Wolsey was taking care of the exchequer, the chancery and, to a great extent, international diplomacy. Having been responsible for supplying and equipping the army in France, Wolsey had a key role in negotiating the Anglo-French peace treaty of 1514, but his crowning triumph was stage-managing the extravaganza of the Field of Cloth of Gold and the subsequent negotiations. Much of the tripartite negotiation between England, France and the Holy Roman Emperor was conducted by Wolsey in Henry's name. At the same time as establishing himself as the power behind the throne, Wolsey was making his way speedily up the ranks of the church. In one year, 1514, he became Bishop of Lincoln and then of York, and the following year Pope Leo X made him a cardinal.

LORD CHANCELLOR

The office of Lord Chancellor is the second highest office in England, dating back as far as the Norman Conquest. An appointment made by the sovereign, it embraced several functions including that of chief royal chaplain, charged with advising the monarch in spiritual and temporal matters. For that reason, until the late 16th century the holder of the office was almost always a churchman and the Lord Chancellor was often known as 'the Keeper of the King's Conscience'. The Chancellor's judicial duties included presiding over the High Court of Chancery, where cases were determined according to fairness rather than the strict principles of law. He was also the keeper of the Great Seal of the Realm, the seal used to symbolize the sovereign's approval of state documents.

Wolsey had a finger in every pie. His reforms were wide-ranging and mostly beneficial. He revolutionized taxation, basing his new scheme on a valuation of the taxpayer's wealth instead of the old system where everyone paid the same proportion of income. This new income tax not only brought in over £300,000 to subsidise Henry's wars and counteract his extravagant spending, but proved a fairer system under which the poor paid less. It did little to endear Wolsey to the aristocracy, however, who found themselves hard hit. He also made extensive legal reforms, giving priority to the chancery courts, which heard cases impartially rather than deciding them by the letter of the law, and establishing the Court of Requests, which charged no legal fees. He also attempted to address the problem of

Giorgio Vasari's sketch of Pope Leo X appointing cardinals in the Vatican. Being created cardinal in 1515 gave Thomas Wolsey precedence over the Archbishop of Canterbury, placing him in a position of greater power.

land enclosure, which threatened to cause mass unemployment in the countryside, although this proved an intractable problem that would rumble on well into the reign of Elizabeth I.

In his fourteen years in office, Wolsey wielded more power than any chancellor in history, but his position depended on his close personal relationship with Henry. Although his various reforms had made him popular with the working class, his money-raising legislation alienated the aristocracy and his tendency to keep the Privy

Council in the dark about important decisions meant he had few friends at court. Many of the nobles simply resented the spectacular rise of a man of humble origin and envied him his friendship with the king. Ultimately, however, it was his failure to secure the annulment of Henry's marriage to Katherine of Aragon that sealed his fate. But as Henry lost one favoured adviser, another was already in the ascendant. Wolsey's successor in Henry's affections came from very much the same mould and would rise to even greater heights.

Thomas Cromwell

Thomas Cromwell was born into a working-class family in Putney, south London. The family was not grindingly poor, but Cromwell later admitted to Cardinal Wolsey that he had been 'a ruffian in his young days'. Accounts of his early life are vague and contradictory, but we know that as a young man he travelled around France, Italy and the Low Countries working variously as a cloth merchant, a mercenary in the French army and in the household of an Italian merchant banker. These travels enabled him to pick up a broad knowledge of European affairs, both political and financial, and to become fluent in several languages. All this would be turned to good use in his later life.

Around 1512 Cromwell returned to England to study law and by 1520 was firmly established in London's legal and mercantile circles, becoming briefly a member of parliament. In 1524 he secured a position in the service of Cardinal Wolsey and within five years had risen to be a member of Wolsey's council and his most trusted adviser. When Wolsey fell from power in 1529, Cromwell was careful to distance himself from his former master and friend, measures which clearly paid off, as it was soon apparent that he was in good

This engraving of a popular portrait of Thomas Cromwell shows how
fascination with Henry's chief minister continued long after his death.

favour with the king. At the end of 1530, Henry appointed him to the
Privy Council. This in itself was a spectacular rise for a working-class
boy, but Cromwell's star was still very much in the ascendant.

Over the next year, Cromwell gradually took control of Henry's
legal affairs, a job which the impatient Henry was only too happy to
relinquish and for which he rewarded Cromwell lavishly. By 1534,

after engineering the marriage and crowning of Anne Boleyn and supervising parliament's enacting of the legislation necessary to ensure the break with Rome, Cromwell was in all but name the king's principal secretary and chief minister, and by the end of the year Henry confirmed him officially to that position. The following year Cromwell found himself also vicar-general, charged with overseeing church taxation and the dissolution of the monasteries and then, on the resignation of the disgraced Anne Boleyn's father, Lord Privy Seal.

On 8 July 1536 he was raised to the peerage as Baron Cromwell of Wimbledon and the following year received the Order of the Garter, the highest honour bestowed by a monarch. The year 1540 brought him the earldom of Essex and the office of Lord Great Chamberlain. This astronomical rise from humble origins had been achieved largely through his administrative brilliance in modernizing parliament and curbing the power of the nobility, but inevitably it had made him many enemies. His disastrous attempt to secure a fourth bride for Henry, his king and friend, was the final act in his drama.

Meanwhile court life was a shifting and sometimes bewildering dance. As new-made men, Wolsey and Charles Brandon, Duke of Suffolk, were natural allies against the 'old money' represented by the Howards, and Cromwell later found himself in more or less the same position. The Catholic Howards were ranged implacably against the reforming Seymours. The Boleyns stood somewhere between the two, but personally they were at odds with Suffolk and his wife Mary who, as Henry's sister, hated the Boleyns for Anne's betrayal of the king. And so it went on.

*An illustration of Henry VIII attending parliament in the early 1500s,
from the records of Thomas Wriothesley, one of Henry's principal advisers.
Members of the aristocracy are ranged on the right, bishops along the left
side, while scribes can be seen (centre) taking down the speeches.*

CHAPTER SIX

FATAL ATTRACTION

Even among his contemporaries, Thomas Boleyn was a man of ruthless ambition. By 1526 he had two daughters at court and a son working his way up through the ranks of eager young courtiers. Both Anne and Mary had spent their teenage years at the court of Burgundy and then in France, as ladies-in-waiting to the queen, Henry's sister Mary. By the time she arrived at court to take up a place as maid-of-honour to Katherine, Anne was just twenty, with a trim figure, an elegant neck and eyes that were said to be almost as black as her long, lustrous hair. By the standards of the time she was not a conventional beauty, in fact her dark looks were positively unfashionable, but she had a lively and outgoing personality and, according to all contemporary accounts, a powerful sexual magnetism. Intelligent, highly educated, articulate and not afraid to express her views even to the king, Anne arrived at court like a breath of fresh air. She had also been at the forefront of French fashion and her arrival in England had the same impact as that of Katherine of Aragon years before. Women may have

Anne Boleyn's portrait and attire reveals the influence of her time in France.

resented the effect she had on their husbands, but it didn't stop them rushing to copy her elegant attire.

OTHER SUITORS

Henry was smitten. Here was a woman who he not only found sexually attractive but with whom he could talk politics and theology, who answered him back in argument when no one else dared, who teased and took liberties with him. The king's growing infatuation became apparent during the spring of 1526, when he realized that he was not Anne's only suitor. She was also involved with Henry Percy, son of the Earl of Northumberland, and with the courtier and poet Sir Thomas Wyatt.

Knowing he had rivals only increased Henry's passion and made him more determined to win Anne. In the face of Henry's increasing ardour, however, Anne began to draw back. Despite all his attempts, she refused to become the king's mistress. This in itself was remarkable: few women would have had the nerve to refuse the king, but Anne had her sights set on a position far higher than that of the royal mistress. Thomas Boleyn, delighted at the prospect of his daughter becoming queen, encouraged her every step of the way. By 1527, Henry had accepted that Anne would settle for nothing other than legal marriage and a queen's crown. By marrying her he hoped at last to have the son and heir he longed for. The only obstacle was Katherine. He summoned Cardinal Wolsey and suggested that he use his influence in Rome to secure a divorce or an annulment.

A collection of 17 of Henry VIII's letters to Anne Boleyn are kept in the Vatican Library. They were most likely stolen from Anne to provide evidence of her relationship with the king. Though her responses do not exist, the king's letters convey the depth of his attraction to her. Later letters show them discussing the legal processes by which they might be married.

LETTER 4

MY MISTRESS & FRIEND, my heart and I surrender ourselves into your hands, beseeching you to hold us commended to your favour, and that by absence your affection to us may not be lessened: for it were a great pity to increase our pain, of which absence produces enough and more than I could ever have thought could be felt, reminding us of a point in astronomy which is this: the longer the days are, the more distant is the sun, and nevertheless the hotter; so is it with our love, for by absence we are kept a distance from one another, and yet it retains its fervour, at least on my side; I hope the like on yours, assuring you that on my part the pain of absence is already too great for me; and when I think of the increase of that which I am forced to suffer, it would be almost intolerable, but for the firm hope I have of your unchangeable affection for me: and to remind you of this sometimes, and seeing that I cannot be personally present with you, I now send you the nearest thing I can to that, namely, my picture set in a bracelet, with the whole of the device, which you already know, wishing myself in their place, if it should please you. This is from the hand of your loyal servant and friend,

H.R.

LETTER 5

... The demonstrations of your affection are such, the beautiful mottoes of the letter so cordially expressed, that they oblige me for ever to honour, love, and serve you sincerely, beseeching you to continue in the same firm and constant purpose, assuring you that, on my part, I will surpass it rather than make it reciprocal, if loyalty of heart and a desire to please you can accomplish this.

I beg, also, if at any time before this I have in anyway offended you, that you would give me the same absolution that you ask, assuring you, that henceforward my heart shall be dedicated to you alone. I wish my person was so too. God can do it, if He pleases, to whom I pray every day for that end, hoping that at length my prayers will be heard. I wish the time may be short, but I shall think it long till we see one another.

Written by the hand of that secretary, who in heart, body, and will, is, Your loyal and most assured Servant,

H. aultre A.B. ne cherse R

(The A.B at the bottom of the letter was in a heart)

* This means "Either there, or nowhere".

In May, with the king's connivance, Wolsey convened a secret court that charged Henry with marrying his brother's widow in contravention of biblical teaching. Both believed that this would result in a speedy condemnation from the present pope, Clement VII, and an annulment of the marriage. Unfortunately, Charles V chose this moment to attack Rome and take the pope prisoner. It was hardly surprising that Clement, now in the uncertain custody of Katherine's nephew, declined to support Henry's petition against her. For the next two years, Wolsey went on negotiating patiently with Rome.

THOMAS WYATT

Anne Boleyn is thought to have been the focus of Thomas Wyatt's most famous sonnets about faithless women. The mysterious *Whoso List to Hunt* likens her to a deer which constantly evades him in the chase. It ends: *'And graven with diamonds in letters plain There is written her fair neck round about: "Noli me tangere [do not touch me], for Caesar's I am, And wild to hold, though I seem tame."'*
Another ends:
'But all is turn'd, thorough my gentleness, Into a strange fashion of forsaking; And I have leave to go of her goodness; And she also to use new-fangleness. But since that I so kindly am served, I would fain know what she hath deserved.'
Wyatt clearly resented what he considered to be Anne's betrayal with the king.

Thomas Wyatt, over six feet tall, strong and handsome, was a commanding figure. In the succeeding centuries his reputation as a poet has overshadowed his political career but at the time he occupied a significant position in the diplomatic service, active in petitioning Pope Clement VII in the case of the annulment of the king's marriage.

Wolsey's appeal to Rome

Wolsey's appeal was firstly on biblical grounds. He quoted the lines stating that marriage with a brother's widow was unlawful: 'If a man shall take his brother's wife, it is an impurity … they shall be childless' (Leviticus 20:21). Secondly, Henry's marriage to Katherine had required a papal dispensation, and Wolsey maintained that Pope Julius had exceeded his powers in granting that dispensation, thus making it unlawful. This, of course, went further than the immediate concern over the marriage, as it constituted a direct and more general challenge to papal authority. Wolsey also sought an agreement that the case should be decided by a court in England, thus ensuring that he, as papal legate, would be able to influence the verdict.

In June 1529, a court finally convened in London. Wolsey was to be joined by another papal legate, Cardinal Campeggio, but he took a long time to arrive and then delayed proceedings for weeks. When the sitting finally got under way Katherine, who had initially been kept in the dark about Henry's plans to divorce her, appeared in court to declare her intention to appeal to Rome. At the papal hearing at Blackfriars in 1529, Katherine of Aragon made an impassioned speech. 'Sir, I beseech you for all the love that hath been between us, and for the love of God, let me have justice. Take of me some pity and compassion, for I am a poor woman, and a stranger born out of your dominion. I have here no assured friends, and much less impartial counsel. … Alas! Sir, wherein have I offended you, or what occasion of displeasure have I deserved? … I have been to you a true, humble and obedient wife, ever comfortable to your will and pleasure, that never said or did any thing to the contrary thereof, being always well pleased and contented with all things wherein you had any delight or dalliance, whether it were in little or much.'

The court was adjourned and before it could be reconvened the pope signed an alliance with Charles V and announced that in response to Katherine's appeal, the case was to be transferred to Rome. This was clearly going to be a long struggle, and one for which Henry had no time. Wolsey's usual method of careful diplomacy had failed him and he had failed the king. In his anger and frustration, and egged on by the Boleyn faction, Henry placed the blame for all this delay squarely on his old adviser. Wolsey's ultimate fate had been sealed.

THE FALL OF WOLSEY

During fifteen years of faithful service to Henry, Wolsey had seen the king's anger directed at other unfortunates and had connived at the downfall of many. Now it was his turn. In October 1529 he was indicted of praemunire, or challenging the supremacy of the king by supporting papal jurisdiction against that of the monarch. He was stripped of his secular appointments, including the chancellorship – the dukes of Norfolk and Suffolk went in person to demand the surrender of the Great Seal – and of several bishoprics, but was allowed to remain Archbishop of York. Devastated and humiliated, Wolsey was kept under house arrest at his house in Esher, from where he wrote to his friend Thomas Cromwell, begging him to intercede with the king on his behalf. 'If I had served my God as diligently as I did my king,' he lamented, 'He would not have given me over in my grey hairs.'

Cromwell, although genuinely distressed at the downfall of his old master, had his own position to consider and felt his hands were tied, but it may have been through his agency that Henry relented enough to grant a grudging and partial pardon. Wolsey was sent into

virtual exile at York, which at that time was several days' travel from London and as remote from the court as it was possible to be. Barely had he arrived there, however, when he was rearrested and summoned back to London on charges of treason, for which he would certainly have faced execution. On the way he fell ill and, on 29 November 1530, he died at Leicester. It was an ignominious end for a major statesman who, while derided by many for his love of ostentatious display, had guided much of the legislation of Henry's reign and been the tirelessly creative force shaping the king's international image.

HENRY'S LETTERS

During the eighteen months of stalemate, Henry wrote Anne at least seventeen passionate letters. This was remarkable in itself, as he hated putting pen to paper and it is a measure of his growing desperation that he wrote so often to Anne. The increasingly tender tone and content of these letters, all of which end with phrases like 'Written by the hand of that secretary, who in heart, body, and will, is, Your loyal and most assured Servant … ' or 'Written with the hand which fain would be yours, and so is the heart … ' show that they had reached an understanding. Henry would marry Anne as soon as he was free. With Wolsey gone, Henry took matters into his own hands. He replaced Wolsey with Sir Thomas More, whom he had known as a trusted friend since childhood and who he fully expected to support his cause. But in Henry's mind the quarrel had gone beyond the immediate problem of his marriage. His faith in papal authority had been shaken and he was becoming convinced that in matters spiritual as well as temporal, the authority of the king in his own realm should outweigh that of the pope. Initially, More did support him but as Henry's challenge to Rome became more blatant, More grew uneasy.

Holbein's celebrated portrait depicts Thomas More in the regalia of Lord Chancellor, wearing his chain of office.

A letter from Henry to Anne, August 1528 shows the strength of feeling of the king towards Anne:

> *'Mine own sweetheart, this shall be to advertise you of the great elengeness [loneliness] that I find here since your departing; for, I ensure you methinketh the time longer since your departing now last, than I was wont to do a whole fortnight. I think your kindness and my fervency of love causeth it; for, otherwise, I would not have thought it possible that for so little a while it should have grieved me. But now that I am coming towards you, methinketh my pains be half removed; and also I am right well comforted in so much that my book maketh substantially for my matter; in looking whereof I have spent above four hours this day, which causeth me now to write the shorter letter to you at this time, because of some pain in my head; wishing myself (especially an evening) in my sweetheart's arms, whose pretty dukkys I trust shortly to kiss.*
>
> *Written by the hand of him that was, is, and shall be yours by his own will … '*

A QUEEN IN EXILE

In 1531, Henry publicly repudiated his wife of 22 years. Katherine was banished from court and stripped of her title, henceforth to be known as Princess Dowager, a title she vehemently rejected. With just a handful of servants, Katherine was sent to live under guard in a succession of remote castles. Moreover, in a particularly cruel move, her daughter Mary was taken away and forbidden to visit her mother. Although Katherine's upbringing made her naturally compliant to the will of a husband, she continued to insist that her marriage to

Arthur had not been consummated and that Henry was her legal husband: 'In this world I will confess myself to be the king's true wife, and in the next they will know how unreasonably I am afflicted.'

A true princess of Spain, she retained her dignity to the last in the face of all the humiliations Henry heaped upon her. Not long before her death she wrote to her nephew Charles V: 'My tribulations are so great, my life so disturbed by the plans daily invented to further the king's wicked intention, the surprises which the king gives me, with certain persons of his council, are so mortal, and my treatment is what God knows, that it is enough to shorten ten lives, much more mine.'

LETTER OF KATHERINE OF ARAGON TO THE IMPERIAL AMBASSADOR, EUSTACE CHAPUYS 1535

Eustace Chapuys was Charles V's ambassador to England and Katherine's ally against the annulment. On Katharine's request, Chapuys asked Henry VIII if Katharine and Princess Mary could meet. The princess was ill and had not seen her mother for four years. Henry did not refuse the request but warned the ambassador that he feared a popular uprising on Katherine's behalf and that Princess Mary might escape to the Continent. Chapuys reassured Henry that Katherine and Mary were loyal but failed to mention his own attempts to persuade Katherine to support an uprising. Ultimately, Katherine refused to countenance a rebellion hating the idea that others might die on her half as well as disobedience to her husband. Her assurances to Henry that she would never support a rebellion

went unheard and he would not allow mother and daughter to meet, an outcome distressing to both of them.

Mine especial friend,
You have greatly bound me with the pains that you have taken in speaking with the king my lord concerning the coming of my daughter unto me. The reward you shall trust to have of God; for (as you know) in me there is no power to gratify what you have done, but only with my goodwill. As touching the answer which has been made you, that his highness is contented to send her to some place nigh me, so as I do not see her, I pray you vouchsafe to give unto his highness mine effectual thanks for the goodness which he shows to his daughter and mine, and for the comfort that I have thereby received; as to my seeing of her, you shall certify that, if she were within one mile of me, I would not see her. For the time permitteth not that I should go about sights, and be it that I would I could not, because I lack provision therefore.

Howbeit, you shall always say unto his highness that the thing which I desired was to send her where I am; being assured that a little comfort and mirth, which she should take with me, should undoubtedly be half a health to her. I have proved the like by experience, being diseased of the same infirmity, and know how much good it may do that I say. And, since I desired a thing so just and reasonable, and that so much touched the honor and conscience of the king my lord, I thought not it should have been denied me.

Let not, for my love, to do what you may that this may yet be done. Here have I, among others, heard that he had some

suspicion of the surety of her. I cannot believe that a thing so far from reason should pass from the royal heart of his highness; neither can I think that he hath so little confidence in me. If any such matter chance to be communed of, I pray you say unto his highness that I am determined to die (without doubt) in this realm; and that I, from henceforth, offer mine own person for surety, to the intent that, if any such thing should be attempted, that then he do justice of me, as of the most evil woman that ever was born.

The residue I remit to your good wisdom and judgment as unto a trusty friend, to whom I pray God give health.

Katherine the Queen.

Anne gets involved

With Katherine out of the way, Anne became the king's consort in all but name. Keen to hasten the marriage she had so carefully engineered, she began to involve herself in politics. On the death of the Archbishop of Canterbury, she persuaded Henry to appoint Thomas Cranmer, the Boleyn family chaplain, to the position. She was also careful to cultivate Thomas Cromwell, who had replaced Wolsey as the king's senior adviser, and win him to her side. Other prominent clerics who were thought to share Henry's views on divorce found themselves promoted to positions of power. In this letter, written in August 1528, Anne expresses her gratitude to Wolsey and reminds him that she longed to receive good news about the cardinal. 'My Lord I do assure y[ou I do long to hear] from you some news of the Legate,' she writes. '*My lord, in my most humblest wise that my heart can think, [I desire you to pardon] me that I am so bold to*

trouble you with my simple and [rude writing]… My Lord I do assure y[ou I do long to hear] from you some news of the Legate, for I do hope and [pray they] shall be very good, and I am sure that you desire [it as much as I,] and more if it were possible as I know it is not, [and thus remaining] in a steadfast hope I make an end of my letter [written in the hand] of her that is most bound to be.'

Anne then managed to persuade Henry to write as well – and to exert some extra pressure on the hard-pressed Wolsey. *'The writer of this letter would not cease till she had [caused me likewise] to set to my hand, desiring you, though it be short, to t[ake it in good part.] … The not hearing of the Legate's arrival in [France causeth] us somewhat to muse, notwithstanding we trust by your dilig[ence and vigilancy] (with the assistance of Almighty God) shortly to be eased out [of that trouble]. … By your loving so[vereign and] friend. Henr[y R].'*

THE WAR OF WORDS

At the same time Henry was actively pleading his case among the leading powers of Europe, issuing pamphlets and firing off letters canvassing support for his cause. Missives went back and forth between monarchs and theologians debating what became known as 'The King's Great Matter'. The whole of Europe was fascinated by the drama of Henry's situation. At home, a booklet entitled *A Glass of the Truthe* purported to set out the argument against papal rule for all Englishmen to read. It also hinted darkly at what might befall England if a woman were to inherit the throne – as a reminder of how important it was for the king to remarry in order to supply a male heir. Thomas Cromwell, meanwhile, was busily drafting new documents to bolster Henry's authority.

On 5 January 1531, Pope Clement VII wrote to Henry

VIII forbidding him to remarry and threatening him with ex-communication if he took matters into his own hands and disobeyed.

Rome: *'At the request of the Queen, forbids Henry to remarry until the decision of the case, and declares that if he does all issue will be illegitimate. Forbids any one in England, of ecclesiastical or secular dignity, universities, parliaments, courts of law, &c., to make any decision in an affair the judgment of which is reserved for the Holy See. The whole under pain of excommunication. As Henry would not receive a former citation, this is to be affixed to the church gates of Bruges, Tournay, and other towns in the Low Countries, which will be sufficient promulgation. Rome, 5 Jan. 1531.'*

In 1532, five years after proposing marriage to Anne – Henry was still married to Katherine. In the autumn Henry and Anne, who had been elevated to the peerage under the title Marquis of Pembroke, journeyed to Calais to meet Francis I and secure his support. When they returned, it soon became apparent that Anne was pregnant. Suddenly there was a new sense of urgency. A child born before Anne became queen could not succeed to the throne. Sometime around 25 January 1533, Anne and Henry were secretly married at Whitehall. Henry and Anne's private marriage was kept a close secret. There was a rumour that Archbishop Cranmer had performed the ceremony, but he himself strenuously denied this, writing: 'Notwithstanding it hath been reported throughout a great part of the realm that I married her; which was plainly false, for I myself knew not thereof a fortnight after it was done.' In April, Archbishop Cranmer convened an ecclesiastical court to pronounce on the royal marriage. Katherine refused to appear but in her absence the court found that her marriage to Henry was null and void, and his second marriage to Anne was legal. For daring to take this decision

in London, Cranmer was immediately excommunicated and Henry threatened with the same unless he gave Anne up. His answer was a contemptuous refusal and, adding insult to injury, he referred to Clement not as pope but merely 'Bishop of Rome'. An outraged papal court found in Katherine's favour: Henry must return to her or face excommunication.

QUEEN ANNE

Anne Boleyn was crowned queen in a fine ceremony on Whit Sunday, 1 June 1533. On the eve of Anne Boleyn's coronation a festive procession was held in London and members of a German trade guild erected a display based on a design by Holbein, perhaps for a masque, entitled *Apollo and the Muses on Parnassus*, which shows the god and his companions seated by the Helicon spring, a source of poetic inspiration. Various eyewitnesses confirmed, no doubt with delight, that real wine flowed from the cleverly constructed 'spring' until late into the evening.

Her coronation at Westminster Abbey was a grand affair, as a contemporary chronicler recorded: 'Queen Anne was brought from Westminster Hall to the Abbey of St Peter's with procession, all the monks of Westminster going in rich copes of gold with 13 abbots mitred ... and she herself going under a rich canopy of cloth of gold, apparelled in a kirtle of crimson velvet powdered with ermines, and a robe of purple velvet furred with powdered ermines over that, and a rich coronet with a caul of pearls and stones on her head ... and after her ten ladies following in robes of scarlet furred with ermines and round coronets of gold on their heads; and next after them all the Queen's maids in gowns of scarlet ... And when the mass was done they left, every man in his order, to Westminster Hall, she still

going under the canopy, crowned, with two sceptres in her hands, my Lord Wiltshire her father, and Lord Talbot leading her, and so dined there; and there was made the most honourable feast that has been seen. The great hall at Westminster was richly hung with rich cloth of Arras, and a table was set at the upper end of the hall, going up twelve steps, where the queen dined; and a rich cloth of estate hung over her head. There were also four other tables along the hall; and it was railed on every side, from the high dais in Westminster Hall to the platform in the church in the abbey.'

Archbishop Cranmer, writing to Archdeacon Hawkyns in June 1533, noted: 'But now, sir, you may not imagine that this coronation was before her marriage; for she was married much about St Paul's Day last, as the condition thereof doth well appear, by reason she is now somewhat big with child.'

A disappointment

Three months later, at Greenwich, Anne gave birth to a daughter. This was a huge disappointment for both parents, but for Anne, only too conscious of her responsibilities, it was an inauspicious start to her reign. Putting on a brave face, Henry ordered public rejoicing and hailed his new daughter, named Elizabeth after both her grandmothers, as his first legitimate child. Privately, though, he fell into a depression, cancelled the celebratory tournament he had planned and avoided Anne's company for some time. Astrologers and physicians alike had predicted that Anne's child would be a boy. Anne and Henry were so sure that they had already planned the christening. The new prince would take one of the Tudor family names of Henry or Edward. Letters announcing the joyful birth of a son had already been written and had to be hastily amended when

the child turned out to be a girl. In some of them it can be seen that the word 'prince' has had an 's' hurriedly added to read 'princes'.

ACTS AND OATHS

Alongside the personal events the long-running political drama was heading towards its conclusion. In 1534, parliament had issued the Act of Supremacy, recognizing Henry's title as 'the only supreme head on earth of the Church in England' and outlining the considerable powers this bestowed on him. This legislation, largely drafted by Cromwell, marked the final sundering of Henry's ties with Rome and its wording made clear that this was not a title conferred on Henry by parliament but by right. Once the Act had entered into law, all members of ecclesiastical bodies, including the universities, were required to swear an Oath of Supremacy, affirming acceptance of the king's new title and renouncing all allegiance to the pope. Disavowing the Act of Supremacy was to be considered as treason, and Cromwell swiftly dispatched agents throughout the country to witness that the taking of the oath was properly administered. There were to be many victims of this policy.

THE HOLY MAID OF KENT

Elizabeth Barton was an English Catholic nun who, after suffering a serious illness, claimed to have been granted divine revelations about future events. Accounts of her visions spread widely, winning her an audience with Cardinal Wolsey and then with the king himself, who at first looked on her prophecies with good humour. However, during the annulment crisis she began issuing dire warnings about the dangers of divorce, culminating in a prediction that if Henry married Anne, he would die within the year. This began to look more like conspiracy than innocent religious ecstasy and she was arrested, forced to confess to faking her visions and was hanged in 1534. Several prominent courtiers also became dangerously implicated in this affair, including Sir Thomas Wyatt, who was lucky to escape with his life.

The Oath of Supremacy was swiftly followed by a further measure. The Act of Succession conferred the right of succession solely on the children of Henry and Anne, thus disinheriting Princess Mary, who was declared a bastard. In addition to the Oath of Supremacy, all subjects were now required to swear an oath recognizing this Act.

THE KING'S GOOD SERVANT

One of the most prominent victims of the new legislation was Henry's oldest friend, Thomas More. A deeply spiritual man, More was committed to the Catholic faith. He had even toyed with the religious life before embarking on his legal career, and to the end of his life he was sometimes said to chastise himself by wearing a hair shirt next to his skin. He regarded the Reformation as heresy and during his time in Henry's service had done much to suppress the production of a bible in English.

Thomas More

One of the greatest intellectuals of his day, Thomas More was lawyer, philosopher, author and statesman in equal measure. He was also an enthusiastic advocate of the new humanism being promoted on the continent, corresponding throughout his life with other great humanist scholars, particularly Erasmus of Rotterdam, who became a close friend and visited More in England on several occasions. More was a man of surprisingly modern and enlightened outlook, particularly with regard to the education of women. His eldest daughter Margaret, educated at home to a standard higher than that of most men, was often held up as an example of More's open-mindedness.

After qualifying as a lawyer, his service as undersheriff of London established him as a trusted public servant and after a successful diplomatic career in the service of Cardinal Wolsey, More was rewarded with a knighthood and a place on the Privy Council. By 1523 he was secretary to the king, liaising between Henry and Wolsey on the highest matters of state. His grave but pleasant manner meant he was frequently deputed to welcome foreign diplomats and state visitors. When not engaged in state affairs, More retreated to his study and somehow found time for writing. His History of King Richard III, a piece of Tudor propaganda that presented the last Plantagenet king in an unfavourable light, remained unfinished but proved a great influence on later historians and on Shakespeare, whose villainous king owes much to More's characterization. His most famous and controversial work, however, was Utopia, a quintessentially Renaissance work in which he uses an imaginary ideal state to discuss the issues of contemporary society. His appointment as Chancellor, a position for which he was eminently suited, would have been the peak of his career had it not coincided with the acceleration of Henry's split from Rome.

Despite his earlier support for the king, however, Henry's increasing determination to declare supremacy over Rome was something More could not countenance. In 1532 he resigned the chancellorship and was allowed to retire into private life, but he then offended Henry by refusing to attend Anne Boleyn's coronation and by circulating a pamphlet encouraging people to stand by their Catholic faith. Given that he had also narrowly escaped being implicated in the Maid of Kent affair it is remarkable that More was allowed his freedom for so long. But in 1534, when he refused to swear the Oath of Supremacy and the Oath to the Succession, he was arrested and taken to the Tower along with John Fisher, Bishop of Rochester, who had similarly refused to swear.

Fisher had been an outspoken opponent from the start, writing and speaking out against the plans for annulment and appearing in support of Katherine in the courtroom. More on the other hand had wherever possible maintained a tactful and dignified silence. Their sentences were the same, however: both were found guilty of treason and on the morning of 6 July 1535 they were beheaded. More was executed on a scaffold erected on Tower Hill. He is widely quoted as saying: 'I pray you, Mr Lieutenant, see me safe up and for my coming down, I can shift for myself.' His final words on the scaffold were 'The King's good servant, but God's first.' After More's death, Erasmus mourned him as a man 'whose soul was more pure than any snow, whose genius was such that England never had and never again will have its like.'

THOMAS MORE'S FINAL LETTER TO HENRY VIII, MARCH 1534
To Henry VIII. Chelsea, 5 March

Living as a private citizen since his resignation in 1532, More looked for the best in people until the last. This is his final extant letter to Henry VIII in which he petitions the king not to listen to any 'sinister information' that might have been given against him.

It may like your Highness to call to your gracious remembrance, that at such time as of that great weighty room and office of your Chancellor (with which so far above my merits or qualities able and meet therefore, your Highness had of your incomparable goodness honored and exalted me), ye were so good and gracious unto me, as at my poor humble suit to discharge and disburden me, giving me license with your gracious favor to bestow the residue of my life in mine age now to come, about the provision for my soul in the service of God, and to be your Grace's beadsman and pray for you. It pleased your Highness further to say unto me, that for the service which I before had done you (which it then liked your goodness far above my deserving to commend) that in any suit that I should after have unto your Highness, which either should concern mine honor (that word it liked your Highness to use unto me) or that should pertain unto my profit, I should find your Highness good and gracious lord unto me. So is it now gracious Sovereign, that worldly honor is the thing, whereof I have resigned both the possession and the desire, in the resignation of your most honorable office; and worldly profit, I trust experience proveth, and daily more and more shall prove, that I never was greedy thereon. But now is my most humble suit unto your excellent Highness, partly to beseech the same, somewhat to tender my poor honesty, but principally that of your accustomed goodness, no sinister information move your noble Grace, to have any more distrust of my truth and devotion toward you, than I have, or shall during my life, give the cause. For in this matter of the wicked woman of Canterbury I have unto your trusty Counselor Mr. Thomas Cromwell, by my writing, as plainly declared the truth, as I possibly can, which my declaration, of his duty toward your Grace, and his goodness toward me, he hath, I understand, declared unto your Grace. In any part of all which my dealing, whether any other man may peradvanture put any doubt, or move any scruple of suspicion, that can I neither tell, nor lieth in mine hand to let, but unto myself is it not possible any part of my said demeanor to seem evil, the very clearness of mine own conscience knoweth in all the matter my mind and intent so good.

Wherefore most gracious Sovereign, I neither will, nor well it can become me, with your Highness to reason and argue the matter, but in my most humble manner, prostrate at your gracious feet, I only beseech your Majesty with your own high prudence and your accustomed goodness consider and weigh the matter. And then if in your so doing, your own virtuous mind shall give you, that notwithstanding the manifold excellent goodness that your gracious Highness hath by so many manner ways used unto me, I be a wretch of such a monstrous ingratitude, as could with any of them all, or with any other person living, digress from my bounden duty of allegiance toward your good Grace, then desire I no further favor at your gracious hand, than the loss of all that ever I may leese in this world, goods, lands, and liberty and finally my life withall, whereof

the keeping of any part unto myself, could never do me pennyworth of pleasure, but only should then my recomfort be, that after my short life and your long, (which with continual prosperity to God's pleasure, our Lord for his mercy send you) I should once meet with your Grace again in heaven, and there be merry with you, where among mine other pleasures this should yet be one, that your Grace should surely see there then, that (howsoever you take me) I am your true beadsman now and ever have been, and will be till I die, howsoever your pleasure be to do by me.

Howbeit, if in the considering of my cause, your high wisdom and gracious goodness perceive (as I verily trust in God you shall) that I none otherwise have demeaned myself, then well may stand with my bounden duty of faithfulness toward your royal Majesty, then in my most humble wise I beseech your most noble Grace, that the knowledge of your true gracious persuasion in that behalf, may relieve the torment of my present heaviness, conceived of the dread and fear (by that I hear such a grievous bill put by your learned Council into your high Court of Parliament against me) lest your Grace might by some sinister information be moved anything to think the contrary, which if your Highness do not (as I trust in God and your great goodness the matter by your own high prudence examined and considered, you will not) then in my most humble manner, I beseech your Highness further (albeit that in respect of my former request this other thing is very slight) yet since your Highness hath here before of your mere abundant goodness, heaped and accumulated upon me (though I was thereto very far unworthy) from time to time both worship and great honor too, and since I now have left off all such things, and nothing seek or desire but the life to come, and in

Holbein drew John Fisher, Bishop of Rochester, as an ascetic man. Honoured after his death by the Catholic church as a martyr and saint, he shares a feast day with Thomas More.

the meanwhile pray for your Grace, it may like your highness of your accustomed benignity somewhat to tender my poor honesty and never suffer by the means of such a bill put forth against me, any man to take occasion hereafter against the truth to slander me; which

thing should yet by the peril of their own souls do themselves more hurt than me, which shall, I trust, settle mine heart, with your gracious favor, to depend upon the comfort of the truth and hope of heaven, and not upon the fallible opinion or soon spoken words, of light and soon changeable people.

And thus, most dread and dear sovereign Lord, I beseech the blessed Trinity preserve your most noble Grace, both in body and soul, and all that are your well willers, and amend all the contrary among whom if ever I be or ever have been one, then pray I God that he may with mine open shame and destruction declare it.

At my poor house in Chelsea, the fifth day of March, by the known rude hand of Your most humble and most heavy faithful subject and beadsman, Thomas More. Kg.

THE END OF THE AFFAIR

Meanwhile the marriage that Henry had taken almost eight years to secure and for which he had sacrificed so much was steadily deteriorating. Those qualities in Anne that had most captivated him when he had been pursuing her now began to irritate him. What had once seemed like feisty high spirits now felt like wilful disobedience. She was stubborn, capricious, had a vicious tongue and a worse temper; these qualities not only made for a tumultuous private life but also made her many enemies at court. In the wider world she made little effort to endear herself to the people, many of whom remained devoted to the wronged Queen Katherine and referred to Anne as 'the king's whore'. She also acquired a reputation for wild extravagance, spending lavishly on gowns, jewels, horses, furniture and hangings to decorate various palaces. She maintained a household far larger than Katherine's, which included 60 maids of honour and a host of personal chaplains and religious advisers. Worst of all, in Henry's view, she constantly tried to meddle in affairs of state.

Rumours about a split in the royal marriage were rife, but there were clearly periods of reconciliation as Anne became pregnant again in 1534. The child was stillborn, but in the autumn of the following year it was announced that the queen was again expecting. Surely this time it would be the longed-for son? The New Year brought yet more good cheer for Henry, when news came that Katherine of Aragon was dead at last.

Katherine's last years had been sad and lonely. Forbidden to receive visitors, she was kept informed of events by smuggled notes from the Spanish ambassador and from Mary, but she never saw or heard from Henry again. She did, however, write him one last letter in which she forgave him his cruel treatment, begged him to be a good father to Mary and, touchingly, asked him to take care of her ladies-in-waiting after her death.

KATHERINE'S LAST LETTER TO HENRY

My most dear lord, King and husband,

The hour of my death now drawing on, the tender love I owe thou forceth me, my case being such, to commend myselv to thou, and to put thou in remembrance with a few words of the healthe and safeguard of thine allm [soul] which thou ougte to preferce before all worldley matters, and before the care and pampering of thy body, for the which thoust have cast me into many calamities and thineselv into many troubles. For my part, I pardon thou everything, and I desire to devoutly pray God that He will pardon thou also. For the rest, I commend unto thou our doughtere Mary, beseeching thou to be a good father unto her, as I have heretofore desired. I entreat thou also, on behalve of my maides, to give them marriage portions, which is not much, they being but three. For all mine other servants I solicit the wages due them, and a year more, lest they be unprovided for. Lastly, I makest this vouge [vow], that mine eyes desire thou aboufe all things.

Katherine the Quene.

Katherine of Aragon spent her last years as a virtual prisoner at Kimbolton Castle in Cambridgeshire. In those days it was remote from London, and the damp fenland climate damaged her health. Brought low by her years of exile and weakened by frequent bouts of illness (probably cancer), Katherine died at Kimbolton on 7 January 1536, just after her fiftieth birthday. When the news came, both Henry and Anne were overjoyed and ordered celebrations during which little Princess Elizabeth was paraded around the court by her father for all to admire. When Katherine was buried in Peterborough Abbey, Henry did not attend the funeral but had the sense to order a solemn mass at Greenwich at which he appeared wearing mourning. Mary had been denied the chance to visit her mother on her deathbed, and she was not allowed to attend the funeral. Katherine, who had been Queen of England for 24 years, was buried quite humbly as Dowager Princess of Wales.

Henry regrets his marriage

On the day they heard of Katherine's death, both Henry and Anne dressed themselves from head to foot in yellow. This was a curiously ambiguous decision. In Tudor England yellow was a colour traditionally associated with joy and celebration but in Katherine's native Spain it was, along with black, the colour of mourning. Perhaps Anne's fashion statement was cunningly designed to have the best of both worlds, expressing their jubilation under cover of a more seemly regret.

Anne may have hoped that Katherine's death would usher in new hope for her marriage. But shortly afterwards, on 24 January 1536, Henry was thrown from his horse while taking part in a tournament at Greenwich. It was first thought that the king's injuries were fatal and although this proved not to be the case he lay unconscious for two hours, long enough for rumours of his death to spread as far as the palace. When Anne heard the news she collapsed with shock and a few days later suffered a miscarriage. When it became apparent that the child was a boy, Anne became hysterical with grief while Henry, barely recovered from his injuries, was silent with fury. This effectively marked the end of the marriage. As the French ambassador astutely

remarked, 'She hath miscarried of her saviour.' Henry now believed that his marriage to Anne was a mistake and, being Henry, he set about two things. First he looked around for Anne's replacement, and second, he began to search for an explanation for his blunder.

DESIRE FOR EQUALITY

Was Anne the scheming minx that history painted her, or a woman out of her depth in a man's world? She certainly employed her considerable charms to ensnare Henry in the first place but, like many women of the period, she was also to some extent a pawn in the game of family aggrandisement played by her father and uncle. In addition, the constant pressure to produce an heir would have been a strain on any woman. Her unwillingness simply to serve as consort, seen by Henry as meddling in affairs of state, can be put down to her education and upbringing. Whereas Katherine saw it as her duty to serve her husband with meek obedience, Anne's natural ebullience combined with a sound education led her to consider herself Henry's equal in all things, including sovereignty. She wanted to be queen because she thought she had the abilities: marrying the king was perhaps simply the means to an end.

THE JUSTIFICATION

The first part was easy, as he had been making overtures to Jane Seymour for some months and had already moved her into a suite of rooms close to his own. The irony of Anne's situation was not lost on her: she who had cared so little for Katherine's misery while she

was replacing her in the king's affections now found herself being supplanted by Jane. Anne had no intention of bearing the role of wronged wife as patiently as Katherine, but it was soon clear that all her complaints and arguments were in vain. Henry had suddenly realized the cause of all his troubles. Anne, with those black eyes that everyone said were bewitching, had cast a spell on him. She must be a witch, and having used witchcraft to lure him into marriage, what else might she be planning? In the Tudor mind, witchcraft was the default explanation for anything that could not be defined more rationally. Those accused of practising it were usually women and often those who lived alone, who kept a cat or who had any kind of deformity or bodily imperfection. In Anne's case the 'evidence' was that she was unnaturally tall and dark of complexion, and had a sixth finger on one hand. In addition, she was said to have warts on her body that could be interpreted as witch's teats with which she suckled the devil. The obsession with witchcraft begun in Henry's reign would reach panic proportions under Elizabeth and James, prompting several bouts of legislation and, eventually, a book on the subject by King James I himself, *Daemonologie*.

On 9 May, Anne and her brother George were arrested along with four others and accused of conspiring to bring about the king's death. The evidence was that Anne had been overheard discussing her future in the event of Henry's death, and the mere fact of imagining the king's death constituted a kind of treason. In case this curious charge did not stick, Anne was also accused of incest with George and adultery with the other four courtiers. Behind these carefully engineered charges can be seen the hand of Thomas Cromwell with whom Anne, in a typical change of allegiance, had been at odds for some time. How far Henry was complicit in all this, and how much

of it he really believed is not clear, but there had already been gossip at court about Anne's behaviour and now it suited him to believe it. Already infatuated with Jane, he needed to be rid of his wife as soon as possible.

Anne arrived by river at the Tower to hear charges read. Sir William Kingston, Constable of the Tower, recalled their meeting in a letter to Thomas Cromwell: 'On my lord of Norfolk and the King's Council departing from the Tower, I went before the Queen into her lodging. She said unto me, "Mr. Kingston, shall I go into a dungeon?" I said, "No, Madam. You shall go into the lodging you lay in at your coronation." "It is too good for me," she said; "Jesu have mercy on me."' By 12 May, all the accused had been found guilty and two days later Archbishop Cranmer dissolved the royal marriage, despite the fact that he had earlier risked Henry's displeasure by speaking out on Anne's behalf.

THOMAS CRANMER'S LETTER TO HENRY VIII, 3 MAY 1536

Pleaseth it your most noble Grace to be advertised, that at your Grace's commandment by Mr. Secretary's letters, written in your Grace's name, I came to Lambeth yesterday, and do there remain to know your Grace's farther pleasure. And forsomuch as, without your Grace's commandment, I dare not, contrary to the contents of the said letters, presume to come unto your Grace's presence; nevertheless, of my most bounden duty, I can do no less than most humbly to desire your Grace, by your great wisdom, and by the assistance of God's help, somewhat to suppress the deep sorrow of your Grace's heart, and to take all adversities of God's hand both patiently and thankfully. I cannot deny but your Grace hath great causes many ways of lamentable heaviness: and also that, in the wrongful estimation of the world, your Grace's honour of every part is highly touched (whether the things that commonly be spoken of be true or not), that I remember not that ever Almighty God sent unto your Grace any like occasion to try your Grace's constancy throughout, whether your Highness can be content to take of God's hand, as well things displeasant as pleasant. And if he find in your most noble heart such an obedience unto his will, that your Grace without murmuration and overmuch heaviness, do accept all adversities, not less thanking him than when all things succeed after your Grace's will and pleasure, nor less procuring his glory and honour; then I suppose your Grace did never thing more acceptable unto him, since your first governance of this your realm. And moreover, your Grace shall give unto him occasion to multiply and increase his graces and benefits unto your highness, as he did unto his most faithful servant Job; unto whom, after his great calamities and heaviness, for his obedient heart, and willing acceptation of God's scourge and rod, addidit ei Dominus cuncta duplicia.

And if it be true, that is openly reported of the Queen's Grace, if men had a right estimation of things, they should not esteem any part of your Grace's honour to be touched thereby, but her honour only to be clearly disparaged. And I am in such a perplexity, that my mind is clean amazed: for I never had better opinion in woman than I had in her; which maketh me to think that she should not be culpable. And again, I think your highness would not have gone so far, except she had surely been culpable. Now I think that your Grace best knoweth, that, next unto your Grace, I was most bound unto her of all creatures living. Wherefore, I most humbly beseech your Grace, to suffer me in that, which both God's law, nature, and also her kindness bindeth me

unto; that is, that I may with your Grace's favour, wish and pray for her, that she may declare herself inculpable and innocent. And if she be found culpable, considering your Grace's goodness towards her, and from what condition your Grace of your only mere goodness took her, and set the crown upon her head; I repute him not your Grace's faithful servant and subject, nor true unto the realm, that would not desire the offence without mercy to be punished, to the example of all other.

And as I loved her not a little, for the love which I judged her to bear towards God and his gospel; so, if she be proved culpable, there is not one that loveth God and his gospel that ever will favour her, but must hate her above all other; and the more they favour the gospel, the more they will hate her: for then there was never creature in our time that so much slandered the gospel. And God hath sent her this punishment, for that she feignedly hath professed his gospel in her mouth, and not in heart and deed. And though she have offended so, that she hath deserved never to be reconciled unto your Grace's favour; yet Almighty God hath manifoldly declared his goodness towards your Grace, and never offended you. But your Grace, I am sure, acknowledgeth that you have offended him. Wherefore, I trust that your Grace will bear no less entire favour unto the truth of the gospel than you did before: forsomuch as your Grace's favour to the gospel was not led by affection unto her, but by zeal unto the truth.

And thus I beseech Almighty God, whose gospel he hath ordained your Grace to be defender of, ever to preserve your Grace from all evil, and give you at the end the promise of his gospel. From Lambeth, the 3d day of May.

After I had written this letter unto your Grace, my Lord Chancellor, my Lord Oxford, my Lord of Sussex, and my Lord Chamberlain of your Grace's house, sent for me to come unto the Star-Chamber; and there declared unto me such things as your Grace's pleasure was they should make me privy unto. For the which I am most bounden unto your Grace. And what communication we had together, I doubt not but they will make the true report thereof unto your Grace. I am exceedingly sorry that such faults can be proved by the Queen, as I heard of their relation.

But I am, and ever shall be, your faithful subject.

On 17 May, George Boleyn and the other four men were executed and two days later Anne herself was led to the scaffold where she gave the following speech:

> *'I am come hither to accuse no man, nor to speak anything of that, whereof I am accused and condemned to die, but I pray God save the king and send him long to reign over you, for a gentler nor a more merciful prince was there never: and to me he was ever a good, a gentle and sovereign lord. And if any person will meddle of my cause, I require them to judge the best. And thus I take my leave of the world and of you all, and I heartily desire you all to pray for me.'*

Her execution was witnessed by Thomas Cromwell, the Lord Mayor and most of the Privy Council, as well as members of the nobility.

Henry was not among them, and he did not decree a royal funeral. With the fall of Anne, the fortunes of the entire Boleyn family went into decline. Thomas Boleyn somehow managed to retain his position at court but the terrible deaths of his daughter and son had left him a broken man. His wife died, many said of a broken heart, within a year of her daughter's execution and he himself followed shortly afterwards. Mary, Henry's ex-mistress, died in 1542. Eight years after Anne's coronation, not a single member of the immediate Boleyn family remained.

GENTLE JANE

The day after Anne's execution, Henry announced his betrothal to Jane Seymour. Ten days later they were married quietly at Whitehall by Archbishop Cranmer. The Seymours were a prominent aristocratic family whose family motto 'Bound to obey and serve' seems to sum up Jane's life. By the time Henry began to take an interest, Jane was approaching spinsterhood. At 27 she had been at court for at least six years, serving first Katherine of Aragon and then Anne Boleyn without attracting much attention. Chapuys, the French ambassador, wrote that 'she is of middle height and nobody thinks that she has much beauty. Her complexion is so whitish that she may be called rather pale … she is not very intelligent and is said to be rather haughty.' Like the Boleyns, to whom they were distantly related, the Seymours profited hugely from their daughter's advancement.

After the passionate Anne, Jane came as a blessed relief. She was the opposite of Anne in every respect, including appearance. Where Anne had been tall, dark and lively, Jane was pale, fair and reserved. Anne's bright intellect had been honed by a classical education

Holbein's portrait of a rather prim-faced Jane Seymour gives little idea of the attraction she held for Henry. Elegantly yet quite plainly dressed, she has her hair completely covered and wears what was by then a somewhat old-fashioned Tudor gable headdress. She looks more like a respectable merchant's wife than a potential queen.

but Jane, although she could read and write, was not especially well educated and preferred the wifely pursuits of needlework and household management. For Henry she was the peaceful refuge he needed. They settled down to a quiet life, mostly at Hampton Court, and under Queen Jane the whole character of court life changed. Out went the gaiety, the lavish entertainments and the extravagant spending of Anne's reign, but out too went many of the dangerous intrigues that had so poisoned the atmosphere of the court. A new sense of decorum reigned, enforced by strict rules governing behaviour and dress. The French fashions beloved by Anne were replaced by English gowns, still richly embellished but more conservative in style. As Sir John Russell noted, 'the richer queen Jane was dressed the fairer she appeared; on the contrary, the better Anne Boleyn was apparelled the worse she looked'.

In her eighteen-month reign, 'Gentle Jane' won the hearts of the people in a way that Anne never had, particularly through her kindness to her step-daughter Mary with whom, brought up a devout Catholic herself, she was much in sympathy. Although she failed to persuade Henry to restore Mary to the line of succession, she went a long way in reconciling father and daughter and made Mary welcome at court. Then, in June 1537 came the welcome news that Jane was expecting her own child. This time Henry was taking no chances. He cancelled all her public engagements, settled her quietly at Hampton Court and fussed over her craving for quails. On 12 October, despite a difficult labour, she gave birth to a healthy boy. A joyful Henry dashed back to Hampton Court to see his wife and son and once again set about organizing national celebrations.

On 15 October the long-awaited Prince Edward was christened in a grand ceremony, but a few days later joy turned to concern when

Much was expected of little Prince Edward. The Latin text below this portrait by Holbein reads: 'Little one, emulate thy father and be the heir of his virtue; the world contains nothing greater. Heaven and earth could scarcely produce a son whose glory would surpass that of such a father. Do thou but equal the deeds of thy parent and men can ask no more. Should thou surpass him, thou hast outstripped all, nor shall any surpass thee in ages to come.' To his father he was 'this whole realm's most precious jewel'.

it was reported that Queen Jane was ill. 'Childbed fever' was a form of blood poisoning that affected newly delivered mothers. Virtually impossible to overcome, it was the main cause of maternal death in the Tudor period. Just twelve days after the birth of her son, Jane was dead. A distraught Henry went into deepest mourning, wearing black for four months afterwards. Yet again fate had thwarted him: in gaining his longed-for son, he had lost perhaps the only one of his wives he had truly loved. As he wrote to Francis I of France, 'Divine Providence has mingled my joy with the bitterness of the death of her who brought me this happiness.' Following a state funeral at which Lady Mary was chief mourner, Jane was buried in St George's Chapel at Windsor, the only one of Henry's wives to be given these royal privileges. When Henry himself died ten years later, he was buried beside her. Yet within weeks of Queen Jane's funeral, Thomas Cromwell was on the hunt for her successor.

CHAPTER SEVEN

CHURCH AND STATE

The fact that Henry was ultimately responsible for the greatest religious schism in English history should not be allowed to obscure the fact that for most of his early life Henry himself was a devout man who wholeheartedly followed the teachings of the established church.

He did not set out with a mission to separate the English church from Rome, or to have his subjects ranged against one another in support of the 'old' or the 'new' religion. And he would certainly never have called himself a Protestant.

Declaring the monarch's supremacy over the pope had been largely a means of getting his own way in what was essentially a personal matter, more to do with control than with issues of doctrine. In the wider context of church reform he was responding to currents of thought that were already pulsing through Europe. In many ways, Henry played into the hands of reformers who had far more radical ambitions than he. Finding that he could no longer curb the

Lucas Cranach's portrait of Martin Luther suggests a stocky, perhaps truculent chap clad in sober black. On the day that this former monk, Catholic priest and professor of theology nailed his 95 Theses to the door of a church in Wittenberg, he began a movement that tore old Europe apart.

momentum of what he had begun, he allowed control to slip into the hands of his advisers.

A MAN OF FAITH

Henry's own religious beliefs were made clear in the early years of his reign when his outrage at reading Martin Luther's revolutionary 95 Theses prompted him to write a spirited rejoinder. Luther's work, a root and branch attack on clerical abuses, is widely regarded as the catalyst for the Protestant Reformation that was already sweeping Europe.

Henry's treatise, entitled *A Defence of the Seven Sacraments*, is a spirited defence of papal primacy by a young man who, although he may have had help from Thomas Wolsey and Thomas More, was already an accomplished theologian. In his preface he wrote: 'I hope I have made clear how rashly [Luther] calumniates the Church, and how impertinent, how impious, and how absurd he is against the holy Fathers; against Scriptures; against the public faith of the Church; against the consent of so many ages and people; even against common sense itself ... I beseech and entreat all other Christians, by the Heart of Christ, Whose Faith we profess, to turn their ears away from those impious words and not foster schisms and discords, especially at this time when it behoves Christians most particularly to be united against the enemies of Christ.'

It's hard not to see this outpouring as ironic, in the light of what came after, but at the time Henry was pledging his wholehearted support for Pope Leo X, and for this he was rewarded with the title Fidei Defensor ('Defender of the Faith').

ENGLAND'S RELIGION

Of course, at the beginning of the 16th century when Henry came to power, everybody in England shared the same religion, and that was Catholicism. The church was the bedrock of English society, woven into the fabric of people's lives to a far greater extent than it is today. Its rituals gave dull life a rhythm and its parables and the promise of a better after-life brought comfort to a largely illiterate and hardworking population who had little enough on earth to be grateful for. Lighting candles, touching relics and offering up prayers for the dead were all things people did as a matter of course. The landscape of town and countryside, too, was mapped by the physical evidence of ecclesiastical authority, from the parish churches that saw people's marriages, christenings and burials to the great abbeys and monasteries that had been centres of learning for centuries. Monks and nuns were a common sight and the parish priest was a man of authority. Any attempt at church reform was going to affect the whole of society at every level.

WHAT KIND OF CHURCH?

Perhaps the most crucial problem facing Henry was that having declared himself head of the church in England, it was proving hard to define exactly what kind of church it was. Henry never saw himself as a Protestant. That term was synonymous with Lutheranism, and the revolution being fomented in Germany by Luther made Henry, if anything, stronger in his own beliefs. Besides, he neither liked not trusted Luther himself, who had failed to support him in his quarrel with the pope. Intellectually, Henry was more in sympathy with the kind of Christian humanism promoted by Erasmus and Thomas More, and they advocated reform from within the church, not the institution's destruction.

CHURCH FESTIVALS

Everyone celebrated the major festivals of Christmas and Easter, but in addition there were the feast days of innumerable saints, Lent and Shrove Tide, Advent, Corpus Christi, Pentecost and many more. Perhaps more important, though, for ordinary people, were the festivals that marked the progress of the working year. Martinmas in November brought the hiring fairs, when labourers looked for new employment; Candlemass in February heralded the coming of Spring; 23 April brought St George's Day, celebrating England's patron saint; and the autumn Harvest Festival gave thanks for having grown enough food to survive another winter.

At the same time Henry, well schooled in theology, kept abreast of the latest moves in the debate across the channel. During the 1530s, seeking to escape from the isolation into which he had brought England through his break with Rome, he entered into negotiations with the various heads of the Lutheran states. This necessitated discussion of their various religious positions. Although Henry ultimately found himself unable to accept the Lutheran belief in justification by faith alone, he did start to reconsider some of the central doctrines of Catholicism, including the existence of purgatory and the necessity to pray for the souls of the dead. Nevertheless he still advocated reform from within the church and in this he was generally supported by moderate Archbishop Thomas Cranmer.

Thomas Cranmer

Cranmer was the quiet and undistinguished son of a country gentleman who, having spent his early life in the academic surroundings of Cambridge University, found himself first of all chaplain to the Boleyn family and then, by 1533, unexpectedly appointed to be Archbishop of Canterbury. Cranmer was a cautious and conciliatory character who created little opposition to the king's church reforms, despite the increasing savagery with which they were effected. He seemed not to mind being outranked in the church hierarchy by Thomas Cromwell, whose specially created post of 'Vice-Regent in Spirituals' gave him overall charge of religious affairs. Cranmer was essentially a man of religious conviction who was happy to leave policy-making to others, but despite this he inevitably became embroiled in the factional infighting that characterized the years of reform. Only his long and close relationship with the king, who was always at pains to protect him, saved Cranmer from meeting the same fate as Wolsey and Cromwell. Eventually, though, on the accession of Queen Mary, Cranmer was put on trial for treason and burned at the stake.

The 1530s were years of vigorous debate during which one document after another was drawn up seeking to define the character and the objectives of the new church, but with little success. The Ten Articles of 1536 attempted to set guidelines, but these proved puzzlingly inconsistent, disappointing both conservatives and evangelicals alike. In the following year the *Bishops' Book*, published apparently without Henry's approval, earned his wrath by implying qualified support for Lutheran ideas; this was followed in 1539 by the Act of Six Articles, which sought to clarify the king's position on several key issues. Finally, in 1543, the publication of *The King's*

The burning of Thomas Cranmer from Foxe's Book of Martyrs. Under pressure, Cranmer had recanted his views but then withdrew his recantation and vowed that the hand that had signed it would be first to be punished. At the stake, he stretched out his right hand and 'held it unshrinkingly in the fire until it was burnt to a cinder'.

Book placed the king on the side of the conservatives, although with certain reservations. It's clear that Henry was intimately involved in the finalization, if not the preparation, of these documents. Both they and the surrounding correspondence bear notes in his own handwriting, scribbles in the margin and clear amendments within the text in which he expresses himself quite forcibly. Whole passages in *The King's Book* are crossed out and rewritten – and this by a man who notoriously hated writing.

A BIBLE IN ENGLISH

The next thing on the agenda in Henry's new church had to be the provision of a bible. When Henry came to the throne the bible was only available in Latin, which meant that the largely illiterate congregations could not decide for themselves on the meaning of the texts, but were dependent on their priest to interpret them. This, of course, greatly enhanced the authority of the clergy. While Luther's reformist revolution got under way in Germany, the English scholar William Tyndale determined to make the bible available to the average Englishman in his own language so that each could make his own mind up about the word of God without the filter of church doctrine. As Tyndale told a learned cleric: 'If God spare my life, ere many years I will cause a boy that driveth the plough shall know more of the scripture than thou dost.' Having studied Greek and Hebrew at university, Tyndale had a more profound understanding of the original biblical texts than did the country priests who knew only the Latin version. His call for a bible in English constituted an out-and-out challenge to church authority.

CONSERVATIVES AND REFORMERS

When Henry and his government embarked on the campaign of church reform, religion and politics became inextricably linked, with staunch followers of the old faith lining up in matters of policy against those who favoured reform. Generally, Thomas Howard, Duke of Norfolk, and Bishop Stephen Gardiner represented the conservative Catholic faction while the reformists were led by members of the Seymour family, and included Henry's last wife, Katherine Parr. Policy swung back and forth according to those in power. Under Cromwell, for example, change was implemented with force, but after his death in 1540 official religious policy became more conservative again.

Finding little support for his crusade in London, Tyndale moved to Germany and began a radical translation of the New Testament from Greek into English. In 1525 the first copies were printed in Cologne and from there were smuggled into England, where the work was immediately declared heretical and publicly burned by the Bishop of London, who condemned it as 'pestiferous and pernicious poison'. In 1530, Tyndale's Testament was banned by royal proclamation.

Undeterred, he had already begun work on the Old Testament, translating from the original Hebrew, but he had completed only half of it when he was betrayed to the authorities. In 1536, Tyndale was convicted of heresy and executed by strangling, his body burned at the stake. His last words were reported to be 'Lord, open the King of England's eyes'.

TOO MANY BIBLES

The 1530s saw several candidates for the position of 'official' bible. Myles Coverdale's version drew on Tyndale's original but he removed some offending passages and augmented it with his own translation of the remainder of the Old Testament which Tyndale had left unfinished at his death. At least this version was free from heresy, and Henry was happy to accept its dedication. Barely was it put into public use, however, when another version, written by 'Thomas Matthew', arrived from the continent. In 1537, the 'Matthew Bible' was approved by the king and Cromwell duly organized its printing, only to find

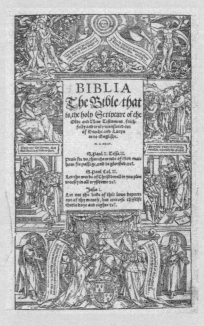

The title page of the Coverdale bible is illustrated with scenes from the Old and New Testaments, including Adam and Eve, and St Paul preaching. Coverdale's dedication to Henry called him 'a better defender of the faith than the pope himself', which caused some consternation, but Henry accepted it anyway.

that 'Thomas Matthew' was a pseudonym and the book in fact contained potentially heretical elements of Tyndale. It was back to the drawing board for Cromwell.

THE MAKING OF THE GREAT BIBLE

Hopeful of putting the Tyndale episode behind him and preventing the introduction of more dangerous Lutheran publications, Henry decreed in 1536 that every parish church in England should have its own English bible. What wasn't clear, however, was which version should be chosen. Tyndale's heretical New Testament was clearly out of the question so Thomas Cromwell, in his capacity as vicar-general, engaged a team of ten bishops to work on a new translation of the New Testament. Tyndale's dying wish seemed to be coming to fruition, but it was soon clear that ten opinionated churchmen would never reach agreement. They quibbled about phraseology, argued theological points and delivered their separate drafts either late or not at all. Three years on, the project was still far from complete and Henry was growing characteristically impatient.

In 1538 another edict renewed the order that a bible be placed in every parish. This gave matters a new urgency and Cromwell, supported by Cranmer, set about organizing the production of a new 'official' version, authorized by the king. But even this was not without incident. Printed in France, where technology was more advanced, it was barely off the press when copies were seized by the French Inquisitor and confiscated. This chapter of accidents finally came to an end in 1539 when the Great Bible – so called because of its enormous size – was printed, this time in England. Production could hardly keep up with demand, and by 1541 9,000 copies had been printed and dispatched to parish churches, where they were to be placed 'in some convenient place' for all to see and some to read. This often meant that the bible was chained to a desk to prevent its removal, giving rise to the common name 'the Chained Bible'. The Great Bible's frontispiece is perhaps its most significant page.

The Great Bible's claim to present 'the content of all the holy scripture both of ye old and new testament truly translated after the verity of the Hebrew and Greek texts by the diligent study of diverse excellent learned men expert in the afforsaid tongues' conveniently concealed the effort and disagreement involved in producing it.

Showing the king handing down the word of God to his subjects, who all cry 'God save the King', it established Henry beyond doubt as head of the church in England, a monarch in direct receipt of the word of God.

REFORMING THE CLERGY

England may have rejected the root-and-branch reforms demanded by Luther, but clearly all was not well with the church. Tyndale had been widely disparaging about the country clergy: 'The priests of the country be unlearned, as God knoweth there are a full ignorant sort which have seen no more Latin than that they read in their portesses and missals which yet many of them can scarcely read … when they come together to the ale house, which is their preaching place, they affirm that my sayings are heresy.' However, it was not only their lack of good Latin that brought the clergy into disrepute. The worldliness and idleness of those purporting to live the religious life had been a target for satirists since Chaucer's day when, in his *Canterbury Tales*, he mocked among other ecclesiastical characters, the Pardoner for his lank hair, reedy voice and effeminate appearance. His clothes are festooned with relics, his crucifix is brass, not gold, and 'in a glass he had pigs' bones … ' The lascivious behaviour of monks and friars, satisfying their sexual appetites in flagrant contravention of the rules of chastity, was a common topic of alehouse conversation and many priests kept wives and families more or less openly. Even Cardinal Wolsey made little secret of the fact that for over a decade he lived in a 'non-canonical' marriage with a woman called Joan Larke, with whom he had two children.

Another commonly held resentment was that by withdrawing from the world into comfortable monasteries, monks and nuns

neglected the spiritual needs of the ordinary people for whom they were supposed to care. The selling of indulgences, already roundly denounced by Luther, was an issue ripe for reform, and another was the clergy's encouragement of what Cromwell's agents named 'superstitious idolatry' – the veneration of relics and the practice of pilgrimage to saintly shrines.

THE DISSOLUTION OF THE MONASTERIES

Between 1536 and 1541, Henry embarked on the one campaign for which history has roundly condemned him. He ordered the dissolution, or suppression, of monasteries, nunneries and all other religious houses, and the confiscation of their assets. Henry was not the first European prince to cast an envious eye over the wealth of his country's religious foundations. Several continental monasteries had already been closed down and their assets seized by cash-strapped monarchs. Henry was, as ever, in need of money for his various military activities and Cromwell was growing desperate for new sources of funding. The church had always represented a potential goldmine, but until now its lands and property had been under papal protection. Suddenly Cromwell saw a way of tapping what appeared to be an unlimited source of wealth under the convenient pretext of moral reform, presenting what was in fact theft as a long overdue redistribution of funds. The fact that most of the funds were to be redistributed either to Henry's exchequer or to members of the aristocracy was not made clear.

RELICS

Relics were body parts or fragments of clothing supposedly belonging to a particular saint, which were preserved in reliquaries and kept on display for veneration. The containers in which relics were held were often more valuable than the objects themselves with some reliquaries made of materials such as chased silver, and decorated scenes from the life of the saint concerned.

Church fathers like Saint Jerome had condoned the practice by making a distinction between veneration and worship: 'We do not worship, we do not adore, for fear that we should bow down to the creature rather than to the creator, but we venerate the relics of the martyrs in order the better to adore him whose martyrs they are.' However, by the 16th century people had begun to regard the object itself as a means of working miracles, particularly to cure ailments. (This was regarded by reformers as blasphemy.) Furthermore, the clergy took advantage of this need by selling fake relics to the gullible. At every country fair unscrupulous friars would be seen offering anything from a tooth of John the Baptist to fragments of the 'true cross'.

There had been earlier attempts, and on a smaller scale. Cardinal Wolsey had dissolved St Frideswide's Priory, Oxford, in 1522 to form the basis of his Cardinal College (later renamed Christ Church) and followed this by dissolving another twenty small monasteries to provide endowments for the college. Other religious houses suffered the same fate, with requisitioned assets sometimes going to fund

specific projects like Wolsey's and other times to the crown, but progress was slow. There were objections and appeals to the pope, which all took time. By the early 1530s, however, with Cromwell in charge and Henry head of the church, the situation was very different. Now any resistance on the part of monastic institutions could be construed not just as a breach of their vow of obedience but, with a little help from new legislation, as treason.

THE SUPPLICATION FOR THE BEGGARS

This pamphlet, penned by Simon Fish, was one of the catalysts for reform. Fish, a gentleman of Gray's Inn, had been forced to flee London in a hurry after being involved in a play satirizing Cardinal Wolsey. His pamphlet, printed on the continent in 1530 and immediately declared heretical by the Catholic Church, was a scathing indictment of religious practices. As well as rehearsing the usual theological arguments about purgatory and indulgences, Fish urged the abolition of monasteries and the seizure of their lands, maintaining that the church held a disproportionate amount of the nation's wealth while representing only a tiny fraction of the population. Worse, he argued, monasteries not only failed to help the poor in their care, but imposed taxes on them in order to boost their own wealth. By some means or other, perhaps through the agency of Anne Boleyn, a copy of The Supplication for the Beggars reached the hands of Henry VIII, who read it with growing interest and, it was said, 'kept it by him for many years'.

Monasteries and nunneries were usually built in lonely, secluded spots deep in the countryside, guaranteeing peace for their inhabitants. The ruins of Kirkstall Abbey in Yorkshire give some idea of the original grandeur of these monastic establishments.

In 1534 Cromwell, on the king's behalf, began an inventory of the property and assets of every ecclesiastical estate in the country, in order to assess them for tax purposes. At the same time he dispatched agents to 'visit' the lesser monasteries with a view to rooting out the kind of corrupt practices of which Erasmus and others had written. They were also charged with reminding the monks of their duty to reject papal authority and pledge loyalty to the king. These visits came with little warning and almost always elicited the results the

commissioners expected. Brothers and selected servants, interviewed individually, were encouraged not only to confess their own sins, but to inform on one another. Examples of immoral behaviour were unearthed as evidence, sometimes dating back decades. The depravity in some houses was deemed so bad that the commissioners were compelled to close them down immediately, others were forced to apply to the king for their own dissolution.

Some houses were amalgamated, others were closed and the monks and nuns absorbed into houses of the same order. The assets were returned to the crown, on the basis that the monarch had granted them to the order in the first place. The legality of this last measure, however, was not always clear and in 1536 parliament was required to pass the Dissolution of the Lesser Monasteries Act, establishing the monarch's right to dissolve any religious house that was failing in its moral duty and to appropriate its assets. Some houses managed to escape dissolution by opting to pay a fine of around £200, but this was by no means a guarantee that they would be left alone in future. The official word was that these measures were being taken as a matter of reform and with the best interests of the monasteries at heart.

Recycling property

Of the lands and property seized by the crown, some went directly into royal hands and some was passed on as payment-in-kind to various members of the nobility to whom Henry owed favours or wanted to reward for service. Most of the buildings were either deliberately demolished to prevent the monks returning or allowed to fall into ruin. Where demolition was the aim, it was done systematically. Commissioners assessed the building and then

Sir Richard Southwell, a close associate of Thomas Cromwell, was actively involved in the dissolution of the monasteries and became extremely wealthy on its proceeds.

workmen set to work stripping lead from the roof, pulling down the drainpipes and melting down the lead for pig-iron. The bells were pulled down and broken up with sledgehammers, to be sold or melted down. Furniture and less valuable movables were then sold off at auction to the highest bidder. Any building left vacant was either converted into housing or, more usually, used as a quarry by aspiring local landowners who raided it for stones to rebuild or extend their manor houses. England's rich heritage of medieval statuary and church decoration was lost or defaced during the years of violent 'reform'. Much of what was left would be vandalized by Puritan iconoclasts during the civil war of the 17th century.

THE PILGRIMAGE OF GRACE

The dissolution of monasteries generated one of the few genuinely threatening episodes of Henry's reign. In 1536, the dissolution campaign was well under way, but if Henry thought the people would support it he was much mistaken. Throughout the country there were rumblings of discontent. For the average Englishman, an attack on his religion was a threat to his whole way of life. People did not want their parish church robbed of its treasures, they objected to being told how they should worship and were far from convinced by the cover story about moral reform. The nobility, more prosaically, were growing nervous in case Henry, realizing how easy it was to seize the church's lands, might next turn his attention to their own estates. In addition, most people rightly saw Cromwell's hand behind these policies, which only added to the mistrust in which he was held. Many had never forgiven him for his betrayal of their beloved Katherine of Aragon and blamed him for misleading the king, while the aristocracy resented the rise of what they regarded as this base-born upstart. There were, too, pockets of local unrest fuelled by rising food prices. It added up to a tinderbox of discontent.

The Pilgrimage of Grace began as a peaceful protest led by clerics opposed to violence, but it sparked widespread discontent and ended with brutal repression. The first trouble began in Lincolnshire in October 1536, shortly after the closing of the local abbey. Led by a monk and a shoemaker, a force of 20,000 demonstrators marched on Lincoln and occupied the cathedral. Although they had the support of local gentry, they were mostly working people demanding the freedom to worship in the traditional way and protesting against the confiscation of treasures from their local churches. They only disbanded when Henry, alarmed at any hint of insurrection, threatened to send in the troops under Charles Brandon. The Lincolnshire Rising was a fairly low-key affair and easily contained, but it was the curtain-raiser for a real drama.

The north of England was conservative by nature and would remain a bastion of the Catholic faith well into the reigns of Henry's successors. A few days after the Lincolnshire protests were put down, trouble broke out in York. Robert Aske was the lawyer son of an old and well-connected Yorkshire family. A devout man and opposed to Henry's religious reforms, he took up the cause of the local rebels and, by 10 October 1536, was acknowledged as their leader.

He proved a charismatic commander and with funding from local landowners managed to transform a rabble into a well-drilled and disciplined fighting force. With Aske at their head and marching under the banner of the Five Wounds of Christ, 9,000 men entered York and occupied the city. The proclamation of the Pilgrimage was affixed to the door of York Minster. It maintained 'that their insurrection should extend no further than to the maintenance and

defence of the faith of Christ and the deliverance of holy church, sore decayed and oppressed, and to the furtherance also of private and public matters in the realm concerning the wealth of all the king's poor subjects.'

Referring to their movement as the Pilgrimage of Grace, they sanctioned the renewal of Catholic worship, drove out the king's tenants from the church properties they had newly occupied and reinstated the monks and nuns.

By the end of October they had taken Pontefract Castle and their ranks had swollen to 35,000 men. This was clearly no local uprising but a serious threat to the state and the Duke of Norfolk was swiftly dispatched to deal with it. At Doncaster, finding Aske's much larger forces ranged against him, Norfolk backed down and opened negotiations. In the king's name he promised that the abbeys would be reprieved until a regional parliament, to be held at York within the year, had met. In the meantime, the king would consider their grievances.

Fountains Abbey in Yorkshire is one of the best preserved of the monastic ruins. Home to a Cistercian community for 400 years, it was the centre of some underhand dealings before its dissolution. In 1536 the abbot, William Thirsk, was denounced to the royal commissioners for immorality by one of the monks, Marmaduke Bradley, who then bribed the commissioners with 600 marks to be allowed to replace Thirsk as abbot. His triumph was short-lived, however: just three years later he was forced to surrender the abbey to the crown.

On these assurances Aske dismissed his followers and set off for London. He was on his way back to York, under safe conduct and with promises of redress, when fighting broke out again in the north.

Infuriated, Henry went back on his word. Aske was seized, convicted of high treason and imprisoned in the Tower, before being taken back to York and executed on 12 July 1537. His body was hanged in chains from the walls of York castle as a warning to other would-be rebels. Over the next weeks, 216 executions took place as knights and lords, abbots and parish priests from the northern counties were all rooted out and hanged or beheaded. Henry's vengeance was once again seen to be swift and brutal.

A SECOND WAVE OF SUPPRESSION

Henry and Cromwell continued to maintain that their aim was reform, but from the summer of 1537 it was becoming clear that the real objective was the complete destruction of the monastic way of life in England. Now, however, instead of having the closure inflicted on them, religious houses were required to 'surrender' voluntarily. Legislation was drawn up naming the head of each religious foundation as the 'owner' of its property and assets. In the event of that owner being convicted of treason, the assets of the house would revert to the crown. Cromwell also offered life pensions to those monks who cooperated. This resulted in many of them pressing their abbots to apply for dissolution. At the same time, the abbots knew that a refusal to surrender might well result in a charge of treason, which would mean their house would be dissolved anyway. Cromwell had the case neatly sewn up.

Although there were minor concessions after the Pilgrimage of Grace, the dissolution of monasteries continued unabated and resistance met with brutal suppression. The monks of Hexham Abbey in Northumberland, who tried to resist Cromwell's commissioners by force, were executed on Henry's personal orders. By 1539, almost

Fountains Abbey in Yorkshire is one of the best preserved of the monastic ruins. Home to a Cistercian community for 400 years, it was the centre of some underhand dealings before its dissolution. In 1536 the abbot, William Thirsk, was denounced to the royal commissioners for immorality by one of the monks, Marmaduke Bradley, who then bribed the commissioners with 600 marks to be allowed to replace Thirsk as abbot. His triumph was short-lived, however: just three years later he was forced to surrender the abbey to the crown.

all the monasteries of England and Wales had been dissolved. In the autumn of that year, as Cromwell began his final moves to complete the campaign, the abbots of Colchester, Glastonbury and Reading were convicted of treason and hanged, drawn and quartered – an example, if more were needed, of the folly of resistance.

Pensioners

By 1538, Cromwell's carrot-and-stick method had succeeded so well that his department was deluged with requests for 'surrender'. Local commissioners were appointed to deal with the administration and to oversee the providing of pensions, cash payments and even clothing to those monks and nuns who had opted to leave religious life. They were careful to ensure that no one was left unprovided for, to become a drain on the local parish. The average pension was £5 a year before tax, the equivalent of a skilled worker's wage, and this continued even if the recipient found other employment. Nuns were less well provided for, their pensions amounting to £3 on average. Many of them, daughters of well-off households, simply returned to their families, but since they were still bound by their vow of chastity and thus unable to marry, they were often regarded as a burden.

ST BENET'S ABBEY

St Benet's, in Norfolk, was the only abbey to escape dissolution by Henry VIII. The monastery had stood since the 9th century and had witnessed invasion by the Danes and the Normans. Sir John Fastolf, the model for Shakespeare's Falstaff, was buried here in 1459. Instead of closing down the monastery, Cromwell amalgamated it with the bishopric of Norwich and to this day the Bishop of Norwich is also the abbot of St Benet's. Most of the abbey buildings, however, were demolished except for the gatehouse, which can still be seen today.

Catholics under suspicion

As more and more of the old ways were outlawed, practising Catholics came under suspicion. Lady Lisle, the wife of the Governor of Calais and a relative of the king, was just one whose refusal to give up her observation of Catholic rites made her suspect. She was a woman of forthright views who didn't hesitate to express them. In a letter, one of her family servants urges her to be more circumspect: 'I first protest with your ladyship not to be angry with me but if it might be your pleasure to leave part of such ceremonies as you do use, as long prayers and offering of candles, and at some time to refrain and not speak, though your ladyship have cause, when you hear things spoken that liketh you not, it should sound highly to your honour and cause less speech.'

THE PURGE GOES ON

As the purge went on, other practices came under scrutiny. The possession of relics, lighting candles in front of the altar and going on pilgrimage were all outlawed.

Not only were such physical acts of devotion now forbidden; even the written word became suspect. An edict of 1535 ordered that every reference to the pope should be 'abolished, eradicated and erased' from all books that were to be used in church and even from those used for private devotion. This meant that priceless hand-illuminated prayer books were often defaced and ruined as fearful owners tried to eradicate incriminating evidence. In 1538, when Henry sought to suppress the cult of Thomas Becket, he ordered the priest's name to be struck out of books. The savagery with which these fairly innocuous practices were rooted out and the punishment inflicted on those found guilty are an indication of the way in which Henry's grip on England's church was tightening.

A CHANGED SOCIETY

The Pilgrimage of Grace had indicated the degree of opposition to the new religious laws and the general discontent about the dismantling of monastic life. But Henry's reforms were not just about religion; for better or worse, they affected the whole of society. For example, while reform of the monasteries weeded out corrupt practices, it also created a large number of poor clergy. Monasteries had fulfilled a social function, offering care for the sick and needy and shelter to travellers and pilgrims. Their disappearance meant that responsibility for this fell on the local parishes, which were often unable or unwilling to cope.

Similarly, while the outlawing of superstitious practices cleared the way for more intellectual honesty in religion, it robbed the majority of uneducated people of their simple spiritual comforts and left them fearful. There were also more subtle long-term changes that would gradually turn England into a more secular society. The church had always been regarded as a suitable and not very demanding career for the younger sons of the nobility. Many went into the church not because they had a religious vocation but because government appointments were traditionally reserved for churchmen and a clerical appointment was the first step on the ladder of political advancement.

Henry's reforms meant that becoming a clergyman was a less attractive proposition and consequently more and more senior government offices became the province of laymen. Thomas Cromwell himself had been the first Lord Chancellor to come from the ranks of the laity rather than the clergy and subsequently used his power to increase the number of laymen in authority. This was also true of legal practices: as the church's grip on society loosened,

statute law replaced canon, or ecclesiastical, law in most areas of life. In the economic sphere, Henry's appropriation of the church's wealth shifted the balance of power from the church to the aristocracy, who were the recipients of the confiscated lands and property. Politically, by trying to tread a path between the two extremes, Henry ended up by satisfying neither side and opened up a gap that allowed dangerous factionalism to flourish at court and created division in the country. The king's quarrel with religion may have started out as an attempt to sort out his personal life but it ended by changing the face of English society.

THE CULT OF THOMAS BECKET

Thomas Becket, the archbishop murdered on the altar steps of Canterbury Cathedral in 1170 on the orders of King Henry II, was England's foremost saint and martyr. People travelled for miles to pray at the shrine in Canterbury Cathedral's Trinity Chapel, where his bones had lain since 1220. Those who felt their prayers had been answered left precious offerings. Aristocratic visitors had also donated treasures, the most precious of which was the gold crown of Scotland, given by Edward I. In 1538, at the height of his brutal programme to suppress pilgrimage, Henry ordered the complete destruction of Becket's shrine and even the saint's bones, which were burned. All the valuables were removed to the royal coffers and tradition has it that it took 26 carts to carry them away. Today a single lit candle marks the spot where Becket's shrine used to stand.

Henry, enthroned and holding the orb and sceptre, is shown inside the capital letter of an illuminated manuscript. How he managed to square the destruction he instigated with his instinctive love of beautiful objects has baffled historians.

AN ACT OF REBELLION

Some priests stood up bravely against reformation. The shrine of St Margaret in the parish of Milton near Canterbury had been a centre of pilgrimage for centuries, but when such activities were banned the saint's image was removed. However, on St Margaret's Day in 1542, the celebrant reinstated the image, garlanded it with flowers and proceeded to say mass in front of it. This act of astonishing courage, virtually on the doorstep of Archbishop Cranmer's own cathedral, flew in the face of the reform programme but, remarkably, appears to have gone unpunished.

CHAPTER EIGHT

HENRY'S LAST YEARS

Jane Seymour had provided Henry with the son he needed, but in a period of high child mortality one heir was not sufficient. To secure the Tudor succession, Henry must marry again and produce more sons, and this time he looked abroad. The upheaval of the break with Rome had left England dangerously isolated within Europe and in 1538 the threat of invasion by Francis I and Charles V was very real. Cromwell's advice was that an alliance with one of the Protestant states would be highly advantageous, and with this in mind the search for a suitable bride began.

Cromwell could hardly have been unaware that Henry, not only the architect of a major religious schism but also having disposed of three wives, was not considered a particularly good match. The remark attributed to Christina of Milan, one of the possible candidates, that 'if I had two heads, one should be at the King of England's disposal' may be apocryphal, but it sums up the situation. Cromwell had his work cut out, but nevertheless over the next two years he presented at least nine candidates for approval before eventually settling on

the daughter of the Duke of Cleves, ruler of a small independent principality in the Low Countries.

Hans Holbein was sent off to paint Anne's portrait and, in case she was not found to be suitable, also that of her younger sister Amalia. Ambassador Nicholas Wotton went along, too, to make an assessment of their personalities. He duly reported that Anne was of a quiet disposition, not too well educated and unable to sing or play any instrument (these pursuits being considered rather indecorous in Flanders) although she did like card games. Unfortunately she spoke no English or, indeed, any language other than her own, which was German. He added that in his opinion Holbein's portrait had caught her likeness very well. On the basis of this report and the portraits, Henry chose the 24-year-old Anne.

Perhaps alarm bells should have been ringing. On the face of it, this mousy, untalented and rather dull woman had little in common with the cultured and well-educated Henry who, even in his later years, still liked a little fun in his life. But Holbein's portrait made her look pleasant enough and as Cromwell clearly considered the match politically astute, negotiations went ahead.

A NEW BRIDE

By October 1539, the details of the marriage treaty were complete and Henry was making arrangements for his new bride's arrival. The palace at Greenwich was modernized and extensive improvements made to what would become the new queen's apartments. Oatlands was also being spruced up for its new mistress. On New Year's Day, 1540, Anne's ship finally arrived and an eager Henry travelled down to Rochester to greet her. Tradition has it that he got his first sight of his bride by spying on her in her chamber before making his official

Prince Edward at the age of six was a pale, rather delicate-looking boy with his father's red-gold hair.

entrance, but whether or not this is true, what he saw did not please him. He felt that Holbein's portrait had been flattering, to say the least. 'She is nothing so fair as she hath been reported', he complained to Cromwell, 'I like her not'. Despite all this, there is no evidence that Henry ever referred to Anne as 'the Flanders mare'. It is far more likely that this unkind but long remembered nickname was the result of courtiers' gossip.

The famous portrait of Anne of Cleves shows a woman who is certainly not unattractive but whose face does not betray any hint of her character, which is unusual in Holbein's work. Historians have suggested that Henry was swayed in his decision more by the reports of his ambassadors than by the painting. The portrait of another candidate, Christina of Denmark, was said to have delighted the king so much that he had musicians play while he gazed at it, but he did not choose her.

Hurt pride

One account of Henry's first meeting with Anne suggests that the
royal couple got off on the wrong foot from the start. The king and
his companions, their identities hidden by masks and cloaks, sneaked
into the chamber where Anne was watching some entertainment and
Henry grabbed Anne from behind and kissed her, a bold trick he
had tried on all his previous fiancées. But while his earlier conquests,
obviously recognizing the king through his disguise, had all responded
with girlish glee, Anne had never seen Henry before and pushed him
away, cursing him in German. Although he then revealed his true
identity and a formal introduction took place, Henry's pride never
quite recovered from this humiliation.

Henry begged Cromwell to find some legal way of cancelling the
treaty, but was given to understand that this was impossible without
causing a major diplomatic incident. Despite Henry's continued and
very vocal misgivings, the wedding went ahead at Greenwich on 6
January. But the damage had been done and worse was to come. After
the wedding night Henry confided to Cromwell that, further repelled
by 'the hanging of her breasts and looseness of her flesh', he had been
incapable of consummating the marriage. 'I liked her before not well,
but now I like her much worse', he grumbled. Although he and Anne
continued to live together as man and wife for another six months,
Henry was adamant that the marriage was never consummated and
even began to hint darkly that he could not believe Anne was a virgin.
(The incompatibility of these two claims seems not to have occurred
to him.)

Once again the word 'annulment' was in the air. In addition
to the non-consummation, the matter of Anne's brief childhood
betrothal to another prince was now brought up as evidence that she

had not been eligible for marriage in the first place. Finally Henry got his way, and in June Anne was commanded to leave the court while her husband and parliament considered his position. She went compliantly enough, even agreeing to write a letter confirming that indeed the marriage had not been consummated. By 9 July, Henry's fourth marriage was officially over after just five months.

Man and wife?

Trying to unearth evidence as to whether the king and queen had ever consummated their marriage, testimonies were sought from their attendants. Anne's ladies told how she had given them an account of her husband's behaviour. 'When he comes to bed, he kisses me and taketh me by the hand, and biddeth me "Goodnight, sweetheart," and in the morning, kisses me and biddeth me, "Farewell, darling." Is this not enough?' This has been put forward as evidence of Anne's ignorance and naivety, but it could also be that, realizing the impossibility of her position and wanting to extricate herself from a humiliating position as quickly as possible, she simply went along with Henry's version of events.

Perhaps prompted by a guilty conscience, Henry subsequently behaved well towards Anne, making her a generous settlement of land and properties, including Richmond Palace and Hever Castle, former home of the Boleyns. She was a good-natured woman and once they were no longer married Henry appears to have appreciated her better qualities. She was clearly more intelligent than reports had suggested, and had learned tolerable English within a few months. They eventually settled into a comfortable friendship. Anne was frequently at court and became an honorary member of the royal family, popularly known as 'the king's beloved sister' and was very

In middle age, Henry's shape is even more squat and powerful. Holbein's great portrait, modelled on the Whitehall mural became the source for almost all future portraits of the king.

much attached to Henry's two daughters, especially Mary who was only a year older than the woman who had so briefly been her stepmother. Despite the unfortunate circumstances of her arrival, Anne grew to love England and remained there for the rest of her life. She outlived Henry by a decade, dying probably from cancer in 1557, just short of her forty-second birthday. She was remembered as a kind friend and by all those in her service as a generous and easy-going mistress; she is the only one of Henry's wives to have been buried in Westminster Abbey.

THE FALL OF CROMWELL

Henry may have come to terms with Anne, but he was still brooding over Cromwell's role in the marriage arrangements. Henry's propensity for turning on his closest friends was no secret and in recent years he had become even more irascible and unpredictable, possibly as a result of the head injury sustained in the tournament years before. Cromwell might have anticipated that his role in the fiasco would not go unpunished. Nevertheless in April 1540, while the annulment was still being negotiated, Henry had conferred on him the earldom of Essex and the office of Lord Great Chamberlain, surely signs that Cromwell was still secure in the king's favour.

But Cromwell's years as the king's right-hand man had made him many enemies at court, particularly among the Catholic faction led by Thomas Howard, 3rd Duke of Norfolk, and Stephen Gardiner, Bishop of Winchester. As strong adherents to the old faith, both were implacably opposed to Cromwell and his church reforms and had taken every opportunity to cross him. Until now, Cromwell's relationship with the king had kept him unassailable, while Henry had never quite trusted Norfolk, whose star had been in decline after his involvement in the downfall of Anne Boleyn. At this point, however, Norfolk saw a way to improve the family fortunes. Towards the end of 1539, he engineered the arrival at court of his niece, Catherine Howard.

Catherine was buxom, merry, flirtatious and, at nineteen, already sexually experienced. Norfolk calculated correctly that her youth and vitality would be irresistible to Henry, especially in the face of his current marital disappointment, and Catherine was found a position among the new queen's retinue. Just as predicted, she soon caught the king's eye and by the spring of 1540, within weeks of his marriage, a doting Henry was showering Catherine with expensive gifts, fondling and kissing her in public and, more importantly, making friendly overtures to her relatives. Just at a time when Cromwell might finally be vulnerable, Norfolk's faction now had the ear of a grateful king.

'MANY LAMENTED BUT MORE REJOICED'

On 10 June Cromwell was arrested on charges of high treason. The exact circumstances are unclear but his arrest was sudden and dramatic: seized at dinner after a meeting of the Privy Council, he was taken to the Tower. Within hours of the arrest, the treasurer of the Royal Household arrived at Cromwell's home to seize cash and assets, which were speedily conveyed to the royal coffers, while neighbours thronged the street outside to watch and jeer.

Opinion was sharply divided as to Cromwell's fall from power. As chronicler Edward Hall put it: 'Many lamented but more rejoiced, and specially such as either had been religious men, or favoured religious persons; for they banqueted and triumphed together that night, many wishing that that day had been seven year before. ...

A portrait of Catherine Howard at the age of 21 suggests something of her youth and lack of sophistication.

Others who knew nothing but truth by him both lamented him and heartily prayed for him.' Hall, however, was in little doubt what had brought about the great man's end: 'But this is true that of certain of the clergy he was detestably hated … for in deed he was a man that in all his doings seemed not to favour any kind of Popery, nor could not abide the snoffyng pride of some prelates, which undoubtedly, whatsoever else was the cause of his death, did shorten his life and procured the end that he was brought unto.'

Cranmer's plea

During the next seven weeks Cromwell wrote to Henry from the Tower protesting his innocence, while a shocked Archbishop Cranmer pleaded on his behalf. Letters to the monarch had to be carefully phrased, as neither Cranmer nor Cromwell wanted to appear to be questioning the king's judgement. Cranmer's letter is a masterpiece of evenhandedness, first reminding Henry that Cromwell was a man of 'wisdom, diligence, faithfulness and experience as no prince of this realm ever had. He that was so vigilant to protect your majesty from all treasons that few could be so secretly conceived but that he had detected the same in the beginning.' He went on 'I chiefly loved him for the love which I thought I saw him bear ever towards your grace singularly above all others. But now, if he be a traitor, I am sorry that ever I loved him or trusted him and I am very glad that his treason is discovered in time. But yet again I am very sorrowful, for whom shall your grace trust hereafter, if you might not trust him? Alas! I bewail and lament your grace's chance herein, I know not whom your grace may trust. But I pray God continually night and day to send such a councillor in his place … who for all his qualities can and will serve your grace like to him.'

Cromwell's letters to Henry from the Tower were written with 'the quaking hand and most sorrowful heart of your most sorrowful subject and most humble servant and prisoner', and appealed directly to the king's mercy. He diplomatically avoided discussion of the charges, on the grounds that this would have called the king's word into question.

THOMAS CROMWELL PLEADS FOR HIS LIFE, 12 JUNE 1540

Confined to the Tower, Cromwell wrote to Henry VIII to beg for mercy.

Prostrate at your Majesty's feet, I have heard your pleasure by your Controller, viz., that I should write such things as I thought meet concerning my most miserable state. And where I have been accused of treason, I never in all my life thought to displease your Majesty; much less to do or say 'that thing which of itself is so high and abominable offence.' Your Grace knows my accusers, God forgive them. If it were in my power to make you live for ever, God knows I would; or to make you so rich that you should enrich all men, or so powerful that all the world should obey you. For your Majesty has been most bountiful to me, and more like a father than a master. I ask you mercy where I have offended. Never spoke with the Chancellor of the Augmentations and Frogmerton together at a time; but if I did, I never spoke of any such matter. Your Grace knows what manner of man Throgmerton has ever been towards you and your proceedings. What Master Chancellor has been to me, God and he know best; what I have been to him your Majesty knows. If I had obeyed your often most gracious counsels it would not have been with me as now it is. But I have committed my soul to God, my body and goods to your pleasure. As for the Commonwealth, I have done my best, and no one can justly accuse me of having done wrong wilfully. If I heard of any combinations or offenders against the laws, I have for the most part (though not as I should have done) revealed and caused them to be punished. But I have meddled in so many matters, I cannot answer all.

The Controller showed me that you complained that within these 14 days I had revealed a matter of great secrecy. I remember the matter, but I never revealed it. After your Grace had spoken to me in your chamber of the things you misliked in the Queen, I told you she often desired to speak with me, but I durst not, and you thought I might do much good by going to her and telling her my mind. Lacking opportunity I spoke with her lord Chamberlain, for which I ask your mercy, to induce her to behave pleasantly towards you. I repeated the suggestion, when the lord Chamberlain and others of her council came to me at Westminster for licence for the departure of the strange maidens. This was before your Grace committed the secret matter to me, which I never disclosed to any but my lord Admiral, by your commandment on Sunday last; whom I found equally willing to seek a remedy for your comfort, saying he would spend the best blood in his belly for that object.

Was also accused at his examination of retaining contrary to the laws. Denies that he ever retained any except his household servants, but it was against his will. Was so besought by persons who said they were his friends that he received their children and friends—not as retainers, for their fathers and

parents did find them; but if he have offended, desires pardon.
Acknowledges himself a miserable sinner towards God and the
King, but never wilfully. Desires prosperity for the King and
Prince. 'Written with the quaking hand and most sorrowful heart
of your most sorrowful subject, and most humble servant and
prisoner, this Saturday at your [Tower] of London.'

Against this, however, Gardiner's faction were howling for blood and the appeal fell on deaf ears. Cromwell wrote at length and in great detail, reminding the king of past service and apologizing for any confusion over the marriage, but he had seen enough examples of Henry's ruthlessness to know that his chances of reprieve were slim. In the end he simply begged the king to be kind to his family and ended: 'Most gracious prince, I cry for mercy, mercy, mercy'. But there was none to be had. Cromwell was condemned without trial and beheaded at the Tower on 28 July 1540.

On the day of Cromwell's execution, and just three weeks after the annulment of his marriage to Anne of Cleves, Henry married Catherine Howard at Oatlands Palace. The ceremony was low-key and lacking in the usual pomp of a royal occasion and, significantly, Catherine was not crowned queen. Perhaps Henry was waiting for her to produce a son, or at least to become pregnant, before bestowing this final honour. In all other respects, though, he pandered to Catherine's every whim and showered her with expensive gifts. The royal inventories show that she received pearls, diamonds and other precious gems, as well as gowns and accessories, either as wedding presents or gifts at Christmas or New Year. He also seems to have been touchingly convinced of her blameless character, calling her

his 'rose without a thorn'. In this, however, he was much mistaken. Catherine may have been little more than a child, but she was by no means an innocent.

CATHERINE HOWARD

Despite her aristocratic pedigree, Catherine was relatively poor. Her father was a younger son of modest means and sent Catherine to be brought up, among many like her, in the household of her grandmother, the Dowager Duchess of Norfolk. The atmosphere of the Duchess's London house, from which the matriarch was largely absent, was generally regarded as permissive, with a number of high-spirited young people left virtually unsupervised for long periods of time. As a consequence, by her early teens Catherine had already flirted with and probably been seduced by her music teacher, Henry Mannox, after which she embarked on an affair with the Duchess's secretary Francis Dereham. The relationship with Dereham seems to have been a marriage in all but name – they referred to each other as 'husband' and 'wife' – and they may well have planned to marry. However, when it became common knowledge, possibly through betrayal by a jealous Mannox, Catherine was removed from the household. Her subsequent arrival at court, thanks to the kindness of her uncle Norfolk, was only surpassed by her childish delight when shortly after her arrival she caught the eye of the king.

Both of Henry's previous English queens, Anne Boleyn and Jane Seymour, had been experienced courtiers, rising through the ranks of the queen's retinue and well versed in the etiquette of court life. They were also well aware of the precarious nature of their position as royal consort. Catherine, despite her precociousness, was a novice in this respect, a barely educated girl thrown unprepared into a sophisticated environment in which she was seriously out of her depth. Henry, meanwhile, was giving every appearance of a man experiencing a mid-life crisis. Nearing 50, he was hopelessly besotted with a charming but irresponsible girl three decades younger than himself who, whether she knew it or not, was the pawn of a powerful court faction.

To begin with Catherine did her best to amuse and distract her husband and to live up to her family motto 'Non autre volonté que la sienne' ('No other will but his'), which was conveniently interpreted as referring to the king, although it was more likely to have meant God. Henry, in turn, did his best to keep up with his young wife's energetic high spirits, rising early and filling their days with hunting and entertainments, but the strain was soon apparent. By 1540 Henry was seriously overweight and far from well. At 49, it was hard to see in him the agile, sporty prince he had once been. He weighed 135 kg (around 21 stone) with a 145cm (57 inch) chest, and his slender waist had expanded into an alarming 137cm (54 inches), measurements confirmed by a suit of armour made for him in that year. Years of good living had given rise to gout and recently the leg ulcers that had afflicted him for years had begun to fester, resulting in bouts of fever that left him exhausted and increasingly ill-tempered.

Try as she might to accommodate Henry's black moods, Catherine may sometimes have felt more like a nursemaid than a wife or a queen. She appears to have been fond of Henry in a coquettish, rather careless way, but as the year wore on and the novelty of her exalted position waned, she began to look around her. It was natural that she should be more attracted to men of her own age than to the rather grumpy father figure she had married but, fatally, her undisciplined upbringing had also left her with a taste for romance and intrigue. Both wilful and emotionally immature, Catherine behaved with a recklessness that could only prove her undoing. Girlish indiscretions were one thing: betraying a husband who was also the king was another matter entirely. She took her first risk in accepting her former lover, Francis Dereham, into the royal household as secretary.

A DANGEROUS AFFAIR

In the spring of 1541 Henry fell seriously ill with a fever and there were fears for his life. Catherine was sent away for her own safety and at some point during this period took the opportunity to begin, or possibly resume, an affair with a young man she had met two years earlier while staying at her uncle Norfolk's house. Thomas Culpeper was a handsome and aspiring courtier, already a member of the Privy Chamber and ambitious for further advancement. Catherine had been in love with him in her girlish way, but without any indication that this was reciprocated. Two years later, however, Catherine had greater value, were Henry to die and leave her as Queen Dowager. She and Culpeper pursued their affair under the king's nose for months, although many at court suspected what was going on.

Henry recovered his health and in the summer he and Catherine set out on a grand tour of the north of England with both Dereham and Culpeper in attendance. The word was that Catherine was pregnant and was to be crowned at York Minster, and while this proved only a disappointing rumour, it did suggest that she and Henry were still having marital relations. Catherine must have felt herself safe in her adulterous affair: after all, what the king didn't know could not hurt him. Once back in London, however, the past caught up with her and events accelerated with alarming speed as skeletons came tumbling out of the closet.

A chambermaid from the Norfolk household, who had been privy to Catherine's youthful indiscretions, made these known to her brother. He, a Protestant vehemently opposed to the Catholic faction Catherine represented, wrote a letter to Archbishop Thomas Cranmer. When Cranmer passed the letter to the king at mass the following day, Henry at first dismissed it as a forgery, but he was then shown further evidence in the shape of a letter from Catherine to Culpeper. Recognizing his wife's distinctive handwriting, Henry realized there could be no mistake. He broke down and wept.

CATHERINE'S LETTER

Master Culpeper,

I heartily recommend me unto you, praying you to send me word how that you do. It was showed me that you was sick, the which thing troubled me very much till such time that I hear from you praying you to send me word how that you do, for I never longed so much for a thing as I do to see you and to speak with you ... it makes my heart die to think what fortune I have that I cannot be always in your company. My trust is always in you that you will be as you have promised me, and in that hope I trust upon still, praying you that you will come when my Lady Rochford is here for then I shall be best at leisure to be at your commandment. ... I do know no one that I dare trust to send to you, and therefore I pray you take [my servant] to be with you that I may sometime hear from you ... and thus I take my leave of you, trusting to see

you shortly again and I would you was with me now that you
might see what pain I take in writing to you.
Yours as long as life endures,

Katheryn.

Once an investigation had begun, confessions came thick and fast. Under torture, Dereham confessed his pre-contract to Catherine and their past relationship but then named Culpeper as her current lover. Culpeper, himself arrested and tortured, also confessed. Henry was devastated by these several betrayals. In a blaze of incredulous anger and self-pity, he threatened to kill Catherine with his own hands. He left Hampton Court and took the boat to Greenwich, leaving his wife locked in her rooms. They never met again.

Two days later Catherine, hysterical and terrified of meeting the same fate as her cousin Anne Boleyn, was stripped of her title and taken to Syon House in Middlesex to be interrogated by Cranmer. The Archbishop found his task distressing: 'I found her in such lamentation and heaviness as I never saw no creature, so that it would have pitied any man's heart to have looked upon her.' He suggested that Henry simply allow her to admit her guilt, declare the marriage void on the basis of her pre-contract to Dereham and send her into exile somewhere, but Henry was adamant that Catherine must stand trial. More scurrilous rumours began to circulate about her behaviour, stoking the king's wrath, and while Catherine remained in an agony of apprehension at Syon, her lovers paid the price for treason. Dereham was hanged, drawn and quartered, while Culpeper, as an aristocrat, was beheaded. Both men's heads were placed on spikes on Tower Bridge. But Henry's vengeance did not stop there.

Catherine's Howard relatives were rounded up and executed, including the old Dowager Duchess. Only the Duke survived.

CATHERINE'S CONFESSION

Catherine always denied that she had had a physical relationship with Mannox, but admitted: 'At the flattering and fair persuasions of Mannox being but a young girl I suffered him at sundry times to handle and touch the secret parts of my body which neither became me with honesty to permit nor him to require.' She did however confess that 'Francis Dereham by many persuasions procured me to his vicious purpose and obtained first to lie upon my bed with his doublet and hose and after within the bed and finally he lay with me naked and used me in such sort as a man doth his wife many and sundry times but how often I know not.'

Catherine was eventually convicted of treason and of leading an 'abominable, base, carnal, voluptuous and vicious life', and on 13 February, the day before Valentine's Day, she was taken to the Tower and beheaded. Her final journey downriver to the Tower was borne with dignity. Even her interrogators had been moved by her plight, but she was shown no mercy. Of all Henry's wives, the fate of this girl whose main crime was to be young and foolish seems the saddest. Catherine could perhaps have saved her life by admitting to the pre-contract to marry Francis Dereham. Had that been established it would have rendered her ineligible to marry Henry in the first place, thus freeing her from the charge of adultery and treason. However,

Henry in 1542, aged 51, already looks like an old man. In this rather less formal gown and without the wide-shouldered tunic, he seems almost to be shrinking although in fact he had put on weight.

in her fear and confusion, and deprived of counsel to advise her, she misunderstood the position and thought that to admit the contract would further condemn her. What finally sealed her fate was that in January Henry had an Act of Attainder against her passed through parliament, making it clear that the mere 'intention' to commit treason was enough to condemn a guilty party.

PEACE AT LAST

Henry had rushed into his previous marriages with what many regarded as indecent haste. After Catherine's death he waited almost eighteen months before venturing into another union. During this period he was distracted by the renewal of war with France and Scotland. The king also found himself growing increasingly isolated, both from friends and from his people. The continual unfettered expenditure that had been such a drain on the public finances for most of his reign combined with his religious reforms to make him deeply unpopular with the country as a whole. Even those who were not adherents to the Catholic faith had been troubled by the desecration of church property and widespread seizure of funds.

On a personal level, Henry had allowed himself to be divested, one by one, of all his closest personal advisers – Wolsey, Thomas More, Cromwell – and finally he was betrayed by the wife on whom he had set such store. He became increasingly paranoid and in his frequent bouts of illness began to suspect all those around him of treachery. Belatedly he lamented the loss of Cromwell 'his most faithful servant', accusing his ministers of bringing about Cromwell's downfall by false charges. On 3 March 1541, the French ambassador reported that the king was now claiming that 'under pretext of some slight offences which he had committed, they had brought several

accusations against him, on the strength of which he had put to death the most faithful servant he ever had.'

By 1543, Henry's health was deteriorating and owing to inactivity and over-indulgence he had grown dangerously fat. The leg ulcers that never healed caused him continual pain and made walking difficult. Gone were the days of tennis and tournaments and although he still went riding, he had to be helped onto his horse. Indoors he was sometimes carried around in a kind of sedan chair and pulleys were installed in the palaces to haul him upstairs. Life was becoming increasingly difficult. What he needed at this stage in his life was a companion who would support him in his declining years without causing him any more emotional turmoil. Katherine Parr, a young widow of some means, was exactly that woman.

KATHERINE PARR

Henry's last wife was an extraordinary person. Raised by a determined widowed mother, Katherine learned early on that an independent woman might achieve a decent role for herself in society. Her parents had both been at court in the days of Katherine of Aragon, but her father had died young, leaving her mother, Maud, to supervise the education of three children alone. Thanks to her early schooling, Katherine had a lifelong love of learning, was fluent in French and Italian, and was able to meet Henry on his own intellectual level.

By the time she came to Henry's notice Katherine had been twice married and widowed. Her first husband, to whom she had been betrothed at seventeen, had died young after only a few years of marriage; her second marriage, to John Neville, Baron Latimer, had ended in his death after a long illness during which she had cared for him and two stepchildren with great kindness.

Those two marriages, although generally happy, had been ones of convenience. Now, at the age of 31, comfortably off and with no children of her own to hinder her, she was in a position to marry again to suit herself. Following Latimer's death she had used her influence to secure a position in the household of Lady Mary, no doubt reminding her that she had been named after Mary's mother,

The Family of Henry VIII *mixes portraiture and allegory to illustrate the Tudor succession. Painted in the reign of Queen Elizabeth, it is anachronistic in that, clearly, not all the people were alive at the same time. The enthroned Henry is seen with (left) his daughter Queen Mary with her husband Philip of Spain and the god Mars, who symbolizes the wars of her reign. On the right Edward VI kneels to receive the sword of justice from his father and next to him is Queen Elizabeth, accompanied by the goddesses of Peace and Plenty who symbolize the calm and prosperity of her reign.*

and it was here that she came into contact with both the love of her life and the man she would marry.

By 1543, Katherine was being courted by Thomas Seymour, brother of the late Queen Jane. He was described by a contemporary, Sir Nicholas Throckmorton, as 'hardy, wise and liberal. . . fierce in courage, courtly in fashion, in personage stately, in voice magnificent, but somewhat empty of matter. Seymour was an attractive man, there was little difference in their ages and the attraction was mutual. Katherine was about to accept Seymour's proposal when suddenly the king stepped in with an offer for her hand. Katherine had no particular affection for the ageing king and no desire to become queen, but she had been brought up in royal service. Torn between love and duty, Katherine chose what she felt to be the higher path and agreed to marry Henry. Thomas Seymour was quietly removed from the scene, given a convenient diplomatic posting and packed off to Brussels, where he remained for several years.

Katherine and Henry were married in the chapel of Hampton Court on 12 July 1543. Unlike Henry's last two marriages, this was not a private ceremony, but took place in the presence of both of Henry's daughters and other invited guests. It was as if Henry wanted to make a public statement about what was almost certain to be his last marriage and his choice of queen.

Right from the start, Katherine's strength of character and innate dignity, combined with a cheerful personality, made her universally popular. Having lived both at court and as the mistress of country estates, she had the ability to treat all she met with courtesy, irrespective of their station. She was also shrewd enough to recognize the task she had been given and strove from the outset to make Henry's home life happy and contented. Under her, the court and the

Katherine Parr in the sumptuous outfit befitting a wealthy widow.

royal palaces once more became places of gaiety, but this time without the fevered activity and lavish expenditure that had characterized the reign of Anne Boleyn. Well educated and a good conversationalist, Katherine was an excellent companion for these autumnal years, sharing Henry's love of music and dancing, reading poetry or debating theology with him in private and keeping a company of jesters and entertainers on hand to lighten his mood. Katherine did not neglect her own studies and in 1545, with the king's permission, she published a collection of *Prayers and Meditations,* the first queen of England to publish a work in her own right. But her talents were not confined to the study. She also rose to the challenge of governing the country in Henry's absence when he went off on his final French campaign in 1544, leaving her as Regent.

THE CHILDREN

There was, of course, more to the royal family than Henry alone and, like Anne of Cleves before her, Katherine realized the importance of establishing a good relationship with her stepchildren. By 1544 the line of succession was complex. First in line stood Henry's only legitimate son Edward, followed by any children he might have, and after that any son Henry and Katherine might produce, followed by that potential son's son. Next, in theory, came any sons from a wife the king might have after Katherine, however unlikely this might be, and only then Princess Mary, followed by any child she might have. At the end of this long and convoluted chain stood Princess Elizabeth.

But while Anne had relied on good nature to endear her to the children, Katherine was able to offer intellectual encouragement as well as kindness. Conscious of the importance of her own early schooling, she took in hand the education of the younger children, engaging the top scholars of Europe to supervise the studies of Elizabeth and Edward. A letter from Prince Edward to Katherine makes clear the genuine affection and high regard in which the royal children held their stepmother: 'Wherefore, since you love my father, I cannot but much esteem you; since you love me, I cannot but love you in return; and since you love the word of God, I do love and admire you with my whole heart. Wherefore, if there be anything wherein I may do you a kindness, either in word or deed, I will do it willingly. Farewell, this 30th of May.'

Elizabeth took to Katherine immediately, appreciating at last the presence of a mother figure who was not only affectionate, but saw her own bright intellect reflected in this studious little stepdaughter. In 1545, Elizabeth sent Katherine her translation of Queen Margaret of Navarre's treatise A Mirror of the Sinful Soul – in itself quite a feat for a child of her age – along with a formal but affectionate letter that began 'To our most noble and virtuous queen Katherine, Elizabeth her humble daughter wisheth perpetual felicity and everlasting joy', and was signed 'Your Majesty's very dear Elizabeth'.

Katherine also did much to further reconcile Henry with his daughters. Having already brought up two stepdaughters of her own she knew how to handle this potentially fraught relationship. Judging correctly that she was too close in age to Mary to mother her, she instead did her the honour of treating her as a princess, winning both her respect and affection. It is almost certainly thanks to Katherine that, in 1544, Mary and Elizabeth were reinstated to the line of succession in a new Act of Succession. This overruled both the first Act of 1534, which had vested the succession in the children of Anne Boleyn and disinherited Mary, and the second Act of 1536, which had disinherited and bastardized both girls in favour of their brother Edward. Although the two princesses now had a distant right to the throne, even Katherine was not able to sway Henry enough to let Mary follow Edward in the succession.

A PLOT

Despite Katherine's personal popularity, there were those at court who resented her for her religious affiliation. Like all her generation, born before Henry's break with Rome, Katherine had been brought up a Catholic, but in spite of that she was favourably disposed towards the new faith. It was this that brought her under suspicion from Stephen Gardiner and the Catholic conservatives. In 1546 they made an attempt to implicate her in the case of Anne Askew, a Protestant preacher who was arrested, tortured on the rack and eventually burnt at the stake for her beliefs. The practice of persecuting minor figures in the hope that they might then implicate those more important was a common tactic in Tudor politics, and under torture Askew was questioned about her dealings with 'my lady of Suffolk, my lady of Sussex, my lady of Hertford, my lady Denny, and my Lady Fitzwilliams', all of whom were members of Katherine's inner circle. Although there was no direct evidence against her, Katherine made no secret of the fact that she engaged frequently in discussion of religious matters with the king. Under pressure from Gardiner, Henry gave his consent for a warrant to be drawn up for Katherine's arrest but when things came to a head she managed to persuade the king that her spirited debating of religious matters was only to distract him from the pain of his ulcerous leg. In the end nothing came of any of this but it had been a close thing and Katherine, given the king's increasingly irrational behaviour, had had a lucky escape.

THE END OF AN ERA

In the autumn of 1546 it was clear that the king's health was failing. Queen Katherine had already moved out of her royal apartments to sleep in an anteroom next to Henry's bedroom so she could be on hand if he were taken ill during the night. She was by now more nurse than wife, but her nursing of her second husband during his long illness had prepared her for this and she attended to Henry's needs with patience. Henry, however, faced his end with no such equanimity. Even on what was clearly his deathbed, racked with terrible pain, he anguished about the succession and raged about possible plots and intrigues at court. His main concern was that although young Edward was a healthy lad and showed every sign of making a fine king, he was still only nine and would not be able to rule in his own right for another six or seven years. Henry's will ensured that during that time England would be ruled by a Regency Council, but past experience had taught the king that however carefully he chose the members of this council, his son would be at the mercy of powerful rival factions.

Henry spent his last days at Whitehall, the palace he and Anne Boleyn had designed for themselves in their hopeful courtship so many years before. During the January of 1547 he rallied a little, but even a man of Henry's extraordinary strength of will could not survive the ravages of bodily illness. It is thought that a blood clot from the ulcerated leg finally found its way to his heart and, on the evening of 28 January, Henry died with family members around him. Three days later, on 31 January, his son was crowned Edward VI. Henry's funeral took place on 5 February at St George's Chapel, Windsor, and he was buried, as he had always requested, next to Jane Seymour in the Lady Chapel.

In this allegorical work, a dying Henry hands over power to Prince Edward. Beneath Edward's feet slumps the figure of a pope, knocked out by a book that reads 'The word of the Lord endureth for ever'. To Edward's left stands his uncle Edward Seymour, the Lord Protector.

THE KING AND SYON ABBEY

A grim legend – unlikely to be true – is associated with Henry's last journey. Syon Abbey, by the Thames, was renowned as a centre of spiritual learning and had been much visited by Katherine of Aragon. In 1535, the nuns' Father Confessor, Richard Reynolds, was brutally executed for refusing to accept the king's supremacy and his body placed on the abbey gateway. Many years later, when Henry's coffin was on its way to Windsor for burial, the procession stopped overnight at Syon. During the night the coffin was said to have burst open and in the morning dogs were found licking up the remains. This was regarded as a divine judgement for the king's desecration of Syon Abbey.

Happy at last

After Henry's death, Katherine retired to live quietly at her home in Chelsea. Henry had made good provision for her, decreeing that she should have £7,000 per annum to live on and that, as Queen Dowager, she should be accorded the respect of a queen of England for the remainder of her life. After his years abroad in diplomatic exile, Thomas Seymour was finally allowed to return to England and, when he renewed his proposal of marriage, Katherine was at last able to accept. Katherine and Seymour married in secret in May 1547, but sadly their happiness was not to last. In 1548, Katherine died from the dreaded childbed fever just days after giving birth to her only child, a daughter who was christened Mary.

HENRY'S LEGACY

So, how should the reign of Henry VIII be characterized? Henry's catalogue of achievements is, like the man himself, a tantalizing mix of contraries. For every triumph, there is a downside.

In his favour, he vastly increased England's stature on the world stage, establishing her as a member of the new Renaissance elite, as well as a serious player in international politics and a military force to be reckoned with. On the home front, the idea of a united 'Britain' came a step nearer with the closer affiliation of Wales and Ireland. Henry had also carefully burnished his own image until, in terms of intellect, connoisseurship and political ability, he rivalled any of his contemporaries. In the context of the vast and wealthy European states and their megalomaniac rulers, this was triumph indeed for a small and insignificant island and it created a solid base on which Elizabeth I would so brilliantly build.

But all this came at a cost, and against the bright public image must be set the fact that Henry had inherited an England with a healthy bank balance and he left it almost bankrupt. The lavish lifestyle, the new palaces, the collection of art, tapestries, rare books and so on – all of which were, of course, only what was expected of a monarch of the period – had cost billions in today's money, while the lives of ordinary folk had not improved. Even the vast wealth appropriated from the church through the dissolution of monasteries was largely frittered away. Was this worth the pain the religious 'reforms' cost ordinary people and the division they created?

However, the general populace probably resented their king's personal expenditure less than they did the drain on the economy imposed by the ongoing yet inconclusive wars. In the military sphere, despite his undeniable improvements in the defence of the realm and

the strengthening of the Royal Navy, Henry had not achieved the promised territorial gains in France and by the time he died relations with the Scots were at an all-time low. He also failed to promote foreign adventuring and thus lost out in the race for New World wealth and territory in which Spain and Portugal were pre-eminent.

PERSONALITY DISORDER?

Another factor is Henry's own personality, perhaps most kindly described as mercurial. To friends he was first loyal, then disconcertingly impersonal and ruthless, executing lifelong comrades without mercy. In relations with women he was anxious to please, needy, endlessly romantic, and then cold and pitiless. Recent research has sought medical explanations for all this, from diabetes or a thyroid condition to a rare x-linked genetic disorder that resulted in paranoia and mental decline, while others suggest that trauma in the frontal lobe of the brain, acquired in jousting accidents, led to personality change. Whatever the answer, his mood swings made him unpredictable and, in the end, he was feared rather than loved – a far cry from the golden youth whose accession was greeted with such high hopes.

Personality had an effect on government, too. Henry's impatience with the minutiae of home-based politics led to his putting off important matters and then making sudden, spur of the moment decisions, perhaps without fully comprehending the long-term consequences. At the same time, his tendency to leave basic administration to others frequently resulted in the astute appointment of the right men for the job, especially Wolsey and Cromwell.

NATIONAL UNEASE

Perhaps Henry's greatest achievement, however, was to have defied the highest religious authority and won, breaking the stranglehold of the papacy and giving the church in England the distinct character it retains to this day. These were mighty achievements, yet they inevitably upset the balance of society. The balance of power swung from church to secular, from the bishops to the nobility, while in between the poor suffered through the loss of social care supplied by monasteries, hospitals and so on. Henry had also underestimated the degree to which ordinary people mourned the spiritual comfort of their everyday Catholicism and the division this would cause. His father Henry VII would have been devastated to see the land he had worked so hard to unite once again as divided as it had been during the Wars of the Roses, while in the reigns of his successors the Catholic-Protestant divide would occasion even greater terrors.

Finally, though, Henry's major failure, and his greatest frustration, was his inability to secure the Tudor succession. On his death the country was left in the care of a child and a faction-ridden regency that could only add to a growing sense of national unease and uncertainty. Not until the reign of Elizabeth I, eleven years later, did England regain her equilibrium and self-confidence.

INDEX

INDEX

INDEX

INDEX

INDEX

INDEX